A CAMERA IN THE CAIRNGORMS

by
W. A. POUCHER
F.R.P.S.

*With Ninety-three Photographs
by the Author*

1. THE CLIFFS OF CAIRN LOCHAN

PREFACE

TO attempt to portray all of the scenery of the Cairngorms in one volume would indeed be an ambitious project, for not only is this massive and remote group of hills resplendent with many a spectacle of wild grandeur, but it also comprises some of the finest rivers and forests in Scotland. I have endeavoured to capture many of these scenes in the following pages, but, since the area of the range is so vast, readers may search in vain for some of the places they know. I shall, however, do my best to rectify these omissions in a supplementary volume when transport is easier.

In this book I have described and illustrated only three of the great ascents of the district together with the traverse of that wildest of all British mountain passes —the Lairig Ghru. Whilst these features will appeal primarily to the climber, I have not forgotten those who, for various reasons, confine their journeys to the roads which in the Cairngorms are in very bad shape, especially where they penetrate the fastnesses of the great hills. It is possible, however, to see much of the district in this way, and I have, therefore, included such lovely and easily accessible places as Loch Morlich and Loch an Eilein, together with some of the wild and beautiful glens.

That the Cairngorms will ultimately become one of Britain's National Parks is a foregone conclusion because it is ideally suited for the purpose. The area, however, is so tremendous that even if grouse-shooting and deer-stalking return to their former favour, there is plenty of room for the wayfarer to move about freely in search of healthy exercise, solitude, and beauty without interfering with the sportsmen.

I have, as usual, given away all my camera secrets at the end of this work, and from the voluminous correspondence I receive it is evident that amateur photographers continue to profit by my experiences. This is a very gratifying development in connection with this series of books because renewed interest in this fascinating hobby can only do good to both snapshotter and photographic manufacturer—to the former by enabling him to bring home more pleasing pictures of the scenes of his exploits, and to the latter by finding expanding employment for workers in the industry. If these pages also refresh the memories of those who know and love the district, and at the same time whet the appetites of others who are not familiar with it, I shall have achieved my purpose.

W. A. POUCHER

Courtlands,
Kingswood, Surrey.

CONTENTS

1. The Cliffs of Cairn Lochan — *Frontispiece*

PAGE

INTRODUCTORY NOTES   13
Geology. Fauna and Flora. Weather. Maps. Distances and Times. Centres and Approaches. Accommodation.

GLEN MUICK   24
2. The Linn of Muick. 3. Morven from Glen Muick. 4. Lochnagar from the Spittal of Glen Muick. 5. The Foot of Loch Muick. 6. Looking west to the Broad Cairn and the Head of Loch Muick.

LOCHNAGAR   30
7. The Cliffs of Cuidhe Crom. 8. The Great Eastern Corrie of Lochnagar from the Meikle Pap. 9. The Exit of Red Spout. 10. The Last Rise to the Summit Plateau. 11. The Precipices of Lochnagar. 12. Looking across the exit of Black Spout to Cac Càrn Beag. 13. The Eastern Prospect from the Black Spout. 14. The Summit of Lochnagar. 15. The Indicator on Lochnagar. 16. The Stuic and Loch Nan Eun from the Summit. 17. Cac Càrn Mor. 18. Snow Cornices on the Summit Plateau. 19. Cuidhe Crom from the Summit Plateau.

DEESIDE   46
20. The Linn of Dee. 21. Lochnagar from the Old Bridge of Dee at Invercauld. 22. The Dee at Ballater. 23. The White Mounth from the Dee. 24. The Western Corrie of Lochnagar from Ballochbuie Forest. 25. The Corries of Beinn A'Bhuird from the Dee at Invercauld. 26. Evening at Invercauld House. 27. Braemar Castle. 28. Inverey. 29. Looking west from the Linn of Dee.

BEN MACDHUI   58
30. Ben Macdhui and Derry Cairngorm from Black Bridge. 31. Derry Lodge. 32. Càrn A'Mhaim from the track near Luibeg. 33. Sròn Riach and Coire Sputan Dearg from Glen Luibeg. 34. Coire An t'Saighdeir and Cairn Toul from Sròn Riach. 35. Stob Coire Sputan Dearg. 36. Crossing the last snowfield. 37. The Summit of Ben Macdhui. 38. The Indicator. 39. An Garbh Choire from Ben Macdhui. 40. Braeriach and Coire Bhrochain. 41. Cairn Gorm from Loch Etchachan. 42. Descending Coire Etchachan to Glen Derry. 43. Beinn Mheadhoin from Glen Derry. 44. Looking back from Derry Woods.

GLEANN AN T'SLUGAIN   76
45. Looking towards the Sneck from Glen Quoich. 46. A'Chioch from Slugain Lodge.

THE LAIRIG GHRU   78
47. Desolation. 48. The Devil's Point and Cairn Toul from Lairig Ghru Lochan. 49. The Signpost at Luibeg. 50. Deer at Derry Lodge. 51. The Bridge over Luibeg Burn. 52. Looking back to Derry Lodge and Lochnagar. 53. The Devil's Point and Cairn Toul. 54. Looking north through the Lairig Ghru. 55. Looking back through the Lairig Ghru. 56. The first tree in Rothiemurchus. 57. Looking down on Rothiemurchus Forest. 58. A wind-blown birch. 59. The path through the pines. 60. The New Bridge and Ford from the Cairngorm Club Bridge. 61. Sundown on the Cairngorms from the Dell. 62. Looking back to the Lairig Ghru from the first pines of Rothiemurchus.

Contents

	PAGE
COYLUM BRIDGE	98

63. *Coylum Bridge.* 64. *Grace and Elegance.*

SPEYSIDE 100

65. *The Duke of Gordon's Monument from the Spey.* 66. *Loch Alvie.*

LOCH AN EILEIN 102

67. *Loch an Eilein from the Outflow.* 68. *A birch by the wayside.* 69. *Evening by Loch an Eilein.* 70. *Cairn Gorm from Loch an Eilein.*

GLEANN EINICH 106

71. *The Road through the Forest.* 72. *A lonely Lochan near Whitewell.* 73. *Sgoran Dubh from the last tree in the Glen.*

LOCH MORLICH AND RYVOAN 111

74. *The Three Corries of the Cairn Gorm—Cairn Lochan Ridge from the Outflow of Loch Morlich.* 75. *The River Luineag.* 76. *The Head of Loch Morlich from the Sentinel.* 77. *Meall A'Bhuachaille from Loch Morlich.* 78. *Cairn Gorm from the Head of Loch Morlich.* 79. *Ryvoan —the Green Loch—An Lochan Uaine.*

CAIRN GORM AND CAIRN LOCHAN 120

80. *The Dancing Cascades of Allt Mor.* 81. *Sheep in Glenmore Forest.* 82. *The last old pines in the forest.* 83. *Loch Morlich and Glenmore Lodge from Clach Bharraig.* 84. *Up in the clouds— the Summit of Cairn Gorm.* 85. *Looking down on Loch Avon and Beinn Mheadhoin.* 86. *The spectacular rock architecture of Cairn Lochan.* 87. *The Summit of Cairn Lochan.* 88. *The Pinnacled Summit of one of the Buttresses.* 89. *The cliffs of Cairn Lochan from below.* 90. *Looking back into Coire an Lochain.*

FAREWELL 134

91. *Sundown—Càrn Eilrig from Loch Morlich.* 92. *The Head of Loch Morlich at eventide.* 93. *Rothiemurchus—the shades of night are falling.*

PHOTOGRAPHIC NOTES 138

PHOTOGRAPHIC DATA 141

INDEX 144

INTRODUCTORY NOTES

THE CAIRNGORMS are a massive group of hills rising between the Dee and the Spey, two beautiful rivers which grace the north-eastern corner of Scotland. They are dominated by the second highest mountain in Britain, Ben Macdhui (4,296 ft.), which, although lacking the individuality and superb rock scenery of its peer, Ben Nevis, is nevertheless only inferior to it in height by 110 ft. The group also contains three other well-defined peaks over 4,000 ft.: Braeriach (4,248 ft.) and Cairn Toul (4,241 ft.) in the western half of the range, and Cairn Gorm (4,084 ft.) which stands to the north of Ben Macdhui in the eastern half.

These mountains thus form the largest area of high ground in the country but they do not comprise the whole of the Cairngorms. Outliers coming within their vast scope include Bynack in the north, Monadh Mor and Beinn Bhrotain in the south, Beinn a'Bhuird and Ben Avon in the east, and Sgoran Dubh and the Glen Feshie hills in the west. These tops only just fail to reach the 4,000 ft. contour but even they do not complete the list of summits which merit inclusion in this select company. There is still Lochnagar, the Monarch of Balmoral Forest, and the dominating peak of the Mounth, which, although just south of the Dee, is perhaps the chief glory of the district. It thus commands a place in any work devoted to the Cairngorms and its inclusion is readily acknowledged by all mountaineers familiar with the district.

These vast solitudes cover an area about 30 miles from east to west and some 20 miles from north to south, and whilst they not only well display these many and remote lofty peaks, they also embrace a wealth of river, loch, and forest scenery scarcely matched within a similar compass elsewhere in Scotland. It is more than likely that many of my Scottish readers will think I should here have said the whole of Britain instead of limiting the comparison to the Highlands. But, as they may know, English Lakeland covers approximately the same area as the Cairngorms, and whilst it can neither boast a river having the striking variety of scene displayed by the Dee, nor a peak within 1,000 ft. of the height of Ben Macdhui, it has, in my view, an infinitely greater picturesque appeal. Those who may be tempted to challenge this statement should compare this work with those I have already published on English Lakeland, and, I think, if they are absolutely unbiased in their judgment, will come to the same conclusion. As I have said in one of my books on the Highlands, Scotland excels in scenes of wild grandeur and the Cairngorms are no exception.

There may be some geographers who will cavil at the title of this book, because strictly speaking, the Grampians is the name given to the great mountain range

A Camera in the Cairngorms

running from the south-west to the north-east of Scotland, in which, of course, the Cairngorms are only the central dominating group. Usage, however, has played its part in this nomenclature and all wayfarers, as well as climbers and mountaineers, readily accept it nowadays. It is, nevertheless, a strange fact that the name "Cairngorms" should have been taken from the lowest of its 4,000 ft. summits and is now used as descriptive of the whole region. The older name of the group was Monadh Ruadh because of its red granite formations, so well seen from Speyside by afternoon light. They contrast strangely with the grey schist of the Monadh Liath, which rise to the west of the Spey, the comparison in colour being obvious to the most casual observer.

The Cairngorms are, probably, the wildest and most inaccessible group of hills in Britain and travellers who have not explored them on foot have no idea of their magnitude and remoteness. Seen from the platform of Aviemore Station on a clear afternoon, their majestic western front seems only a mile or two away. But to reach the entrance to the Lairig Ghru, which splits the range, it is necessary to cover eight miles of road and forest track and only two miles can be traversed in a car. On the eastern flanks, however, a splendid road runs from Ballater to Braemar and then on to the Linn of Dee; but the four miles beyond to Derry Lodge, where the road ends, require a strong shooting-brake or a jeep to reach its wild and rough terminus in safety. Even then only the foothills of the major group are encountered and many miles of hard slogging are necessary to bring the walker to the bases of the great peaks. It is impossible to explore the whole range from one centre, and Braemar is the best starting-point on its eastern flanks. This charming village may be reached by bus from Ballater which may be approached by either train or bus from Aberdeen. As will be gathered from this book, Ballater is by far the best centre for expeditions to Lochnagar, since the approach to it is much more interesting than that from Braemar, although there is no reason why a traverse of the peak should not be made in this direction, if accommodation is booked beforehand. Under normal conditions lodgings may be found in both Ballater and Braemar, but at the present time accommodation is strictly limited. The western side of the Cairngorms offers even less facilities to the wayfarer, and apart from the hotels at Aviemore and the Dell in Rothiemurchus, there is little choice. Unhappily there are only six Youth Hostels giving access to the district and they are almost on the fringe of it, a deplorable state of affairs needing rectification, if, as is probable, the area ultimately becomes one of our great National Parks. I shall, however, return to this question later because the paucity of accommodation in the Cairngorms, compared with that in any other similar area in Britain, is veritably appalling.

Before considering other aspects of the range, it seems desirable to mention the Lairig Ghru, a pass whose fame, I might almost say notoriety, is known to nearly every schoolboy. This gigantic rift in the hills provides the connecting link between Braemar and Aviemore and at its highest point the track reaches a height of 2,733 ft.

Introductory Notes

To traverse it is one of the great tests of stamina imposed upon all those who wish to graduate as true "Cairngormers" and its accomplishment is no mean feat of endurance. The distance from Braemar to Aviemore is 27 miles, but a lift to Derry Lodge shortens it by 10 miles on the east and 2 miles can be saved in a similar manner from Coylum Bridge to Aviemore on the west. The net walking distance is therefore 15 miles and those who think a bicycle may be helpful will be bitterly disappointed if they try to use it. The last time I was in the Lairig Ghru, a cyclist was a mile ahead of me and he could not even wheel his machine but had to carry it the greater part of the way over the rough track, which is made more difficult by the large boulders choking it at several points. The approach from Derry Lodge seems endless before the great ravine is actually entered, but that from Aviemore is even more tantalising because the stupendous V-shaped opening is seen from time to time *en route* and the walk through Rothiemurchus does not appear to bring it any nearer. Once the pedestrian has been swallowed up by the tremendous overhanging cliffs his real struggle commences, and, if bad weather adds to the trials of the traverse, he will breathe a sigh of relief when the first habitation comes into view. Those who attempt it should remember that there are at least 15 miles without any sleeping facilities, although shelter may be obtained in the Corrour bothy near the Devil's Point. A stout heart and sturdy legs are essential successfully to accomplish this magnificent mountain walk.

GEOLOGY

The Cairngorms consist of great masses of granite which, in past ages, have been intruded through a gigantic plateau of schists, quartzites, and gneiss. Erosion and denudation have played their part throughout the centuries with the result that streams have deepened the rifts in the plateau, and, aided by the great natural forces of temperature extremes and rain and wind, have created the valleys and shaped the mountains as we know them to-day. To obtain a clear conception of these phenomena it is only necessary to stand on one of the summits to the south-east of the group, such as Lochnagar, when the Cairngorms themselves will appear as featureless hills with flattish tops and rounded flanks, at the base of which the Dee curls its way finally to disappear into the dim recesses of the Lairig Ghru.

The effects of glacial action are scarcely as obvious here as they are in the Western Highlands and Skye, but glacial moraines are evident in many of the valleys and perched blocks can be seen stranded on some of the ridges, one of the best examples being that on the northern slopes of Cairn Gorm itself.

One of the most striking geological features of this range is seen in the deflection of some of the rivers. For instance, Loch Avon was once the source of the Don whilst the original western sources of the Dee have been diverted *via* the Tilt and the Feshie to the Tay and Spey respectively.

Great rock ridges such as Aonach Eagach and the Bidean Sisters above

A Camera in the Cairngorms

Glencoe do not exist in the Cairngorms which, moreover, are also lacking in precipitous rock faces with the two exceptions of Lochnagar and Cairn Lochan. Most of the stony façades are in an advanced state of disintegration and the cliffs have fallen into vast scree slopes. They are now overgrown with mosses and lichens or with grass and heather, and the broad summit ridges are often long stretches of gravel, sand, or shattered rock. However, they occasionally present an unique feature as in the strange isolated tors which characterise Ben Avon and Beinn Mheadhoin. Great horizontal granite slabs sometimes appear on these summit ridges as, for instance, those on Cairn Gorm overlooking Loch Avon, but they are not so impressive as the gigantic Cyclopean walls of Arran, portrayed in my *Highland Holiday*. The Cairngorms are famous, however, for the superb corries which usually lie on their northern or eastern flanks, and at the bases of which rest dark and lonely lochans. Some of the finest examples are those of Lochnagar, Beinn a'Bhuird and Braeriach. Their enclosing amphitheatres of cliffs are scarcely as bold or well defined as those of Coire na Ciste on Ben Nevis, fully illustrated in my *Scotland through the Lens*, but those of Cairn Toul—Braeriach extend for two miles on the east of the Lairig Ghru and present an unforgettable picture when viewed from Ben Macdhui. The larger lochs which add such variety and charm vary from the soft sylvan beauty of Loch Morlich or Loch an Eilein to the wild and barren grandeur of Loch Muick, Loch Einich, and Loch Avon; the last being characterised by its utter remoteness and gloom, accentuated by the beetling and forbidding cliffs at its head.

The distinguishing features of the Cairngorms may, therefore, be summed up as barrenness on the majestic scale, lofty ground covering the largest areas in Britain and a lack of picturesque appeal. But as the mountaineer wanders through and over them he will be captivated by their remoteness and solitude, whilst the immensity of their scale will impress him with a wonder more profound than that experienced elsewhere in our island heritage.

FLORA AND FAUNA

The expeditions recounted in these pages were made during the month of April so that I was too early to see much of the flora typical of the region. I was most impressed, however, by the magnificent forests of native Scots Pine which deck the valleys and some of the lower slopes of the great mountains. Deeside is possibly the most richly timbered glen in the country and Ballochbuie one of its largest primeval forests. Unhappily much of the wood has been felled to provide the sinews of war so that those wayfarers who saw it at its best before 1940 were indeed fortunate. No wonder crowds of visitors flocked to this delectable spot for their week-ends and holidays, for I can imagine no more enchanting place in which to loiter in the very bosom of Nature. Speyside is also richly wooded and the fame of Rothiemurchus has spread far and wide. Although its timber has been felled

Introductory Notes

on several occasions during the last century, the forest still retains much of its grandeur, especially as it is frowned upon by one of the most spectacular façades of the Cairngorms. Loch Morlich is the gem of the range and is enhanced by the trees fringing its shore; but here again the axe has bared much of the adjacent hillsides, thus detracting from its inherent charm. Afforestation, however, has again clothed most of the slopes with young trees which, in years to come, will beautify the whole scene anew. All these forests are carpeted with luxuriant growths of heather, and those on Speyside, in particular, are embellished with juniper, so that the climber traversing these long approaches sees much to soften the austere beauty of the hills. I hope to return sometime during July and August when the immense stretches of heather in full bloom must surely impart an incomparable colour to the countryside.

The fauna of the Cairngorms is no exception to that of the Highlands generally and the red deer provide one of the attractions of the district, especially in winter and early spring, when they are to be seen on the low ground at the heads of the glens. Grouse are prolific on the moors while ptarmigan are common above the 2,000 ft. contour. Eagles frequent the heights and I saw one of them while climbing the ridge of Sròn Riach during the ascent of Ben Macdhui. The curlew, the golden plover, and the oystercatcher are abundant on the lower ground, but snow-bunting and dotterel keep to the higher tops. A friend of mine, Dr. Hendry of Aberdeen, told me he had found six of their nests while making a traverse of Braeriach earlier in the year. Salmon is, of course, one of the great attractions for the angler on Speyside and particularly on Deeside. Walkers passing the Linn of Dee are often fortunate enough to see fish resting on the lower rocks or leaping the narrow falls.

WEATHER

As I have said in other volumes of this series, the mountaineer is dependent on the weather for the full enjoyment of his expeditions in the hills. It is, of course, true enough that if he is experienced he will be able to adhere to his plans and attain any of the remote Cairngorm summits in anything but the most severe conditions. It is, however, an accepted axiom that if he is really to revel in the beauty of scene the most welcome conditions are sunny days with a blue sky and fine clouds. Such delights in these hills do not usually come with the same winds that bring them to the Western Highlands; and, strange as it may seem, it is the westerly and the north-westerly breezes that prove most acceptable. When they pass over the vast ranges adjacent to the western seaboard the moisture is often precipitated upon them in the form of rain, so that by the time they reach the east coast they have lost it all and clear skies result. During my sojourn in the Cairngorms these breezes always brought fine conditions, whereas the winds from the east and north-east were always accompanied by sea mists, drizzle, and low temperatures.

A Camera in the Cairngorms

The Cairngorms are snowclad in a normal winter and the white mantle lasts well into the spring, with the northern and eastern corries carrying snow wreaths even late into the summer. It will be remembered that the winter of 1943 was one of the mildest on record, with the result that snow was a rarity excepting in the vicinity of the highest tops. I well remember arriving in Braemar and observing stacks of ski outside one of the huts. Residents told me that visitors had been there earlier in the year for snow-climbing and ski-ing but they had departed full of disappointment. When conditions are propitious, magnificent snow cornices are common on Lochnagar, Braeriach, and Beinn a'Bhuird, and winter expeditions in these places are some of the finest in the country. Distances are great and conditions so variable that climbers should be prepared for any emergency by taking plenty of warm clothing and especially spare pullovers to counteract the astonishing falls in temperature which may accompany the ascents. An ice-axe may be necessary and is always useful, and, moreover, its use may be *essential* for the safe descent of any of the long snow slopes when it is desired to save time in order to be back before night.

The Cairngorms have attained a certain amount of fame as a ski-ing centre and whilst the well-known hills of the range provide plenty of runs, the best centre is Dalwhinnie, at a height of 1,174 ft., possessing hotel accommodation, where the adjacent hills offer plenty of safe slopes for the enjoyment of the sport.

MAPS

The finest mountain map so far published in this country is undoubtedly that covering the Cairngorms and issued by the Ordnance Survey in 1936. It combines the relevant portions of six of the ordinary one-inch sheets, is contoured at 50-ft. intervals, and coloured on the layer system which clearly shows the peaks, valleys, and ridges at a glance. I think, however, it could have been improved by the inclusion of Loch Muick, Glen Muick, and Ballater, as, according to the present arrangement, it only just takes in Lochnagar and omits its most important eastern approaches. This would have made the sheet rather too unwieldy, but by cutting off the northern strip immediately above Tomintoul and the western edge at Kingussie it would have been brought back to an acceptable size. I respectfully commend this adjustment to the Director-General of the Ordnance Survey for any new issue of this tourist map. Incidentally, the one-inch O.S. map of Snowdonia is drawn on the same lines and incorporates all these good points. These two sheets are indeed a triumph of modern cartography.

If the Cairngorm climber is not in possession of that described above he must use the half-inch maps issued by Bartholomew. Two of them will be necessary —K2 of the Grampians, and K4 of Deeside. The former includes Ben Avon and Braemar, and the latter overlaps as far as the Lairig Ghru.

Every mountaineer visiting this district should also take with him a copy of

Introductory Notes

the *Scottish Mountaineering Club Guide*. The volume devoted to the Cairngorms is edited by Sir Henry Alexander and is full of indispensable information on the whole group. The second edition appeared in 1938 and is of uniform excellence with all the other guides published by this progressive club.

DISTANCES AND TIMES

The remoteness and inaccessibility of the Cairngorm summits must always be borne in mind when planning any expedition, and it is essential to base all calculations upon the climber's own powers. During the early days of a holiday he will not be able to sustain himself for such long periods as at the end of his first week in the district. In order to obtain an approximate idea of the time needed for any particular ascent, it is advisable to base these calculations upon the formula of Naismith by allowing one hour for every three miles of map distance *plus* half an hour for every 1,000 ft. of ascent. This covers the requirements of a normal mountain walk such as halts for food and for viewing the scenery but it does not allow for rock-climbing, photography, or delays due to bad weather, for which an ample margin should be reserved.

CENTRES AND APPROACHES

Under present conditions the Cairngorms are most easily explored on the east from Braemar and on the west from Aviemore. The former village is well placed for access to Beinn a'Bhuird and Ben Avon, although there are no immediate facilities for crossing the Dee without going back to Invercauld. It is, however, a long way from the foothills of the main range, whose approach is made easier by some form of transport. A car may be used as far as Black Bridge, two miles above the Linn of Dee, but beyond that point the road is so bad that even a bicycle is not easy going. If a bridge were thrown across the burn coming down on the east from Meall an Lundain, at present choked with large stones, it would be an easy matter to motor to Derry Lodge. This is ten miles from Braemar but four of them could be saved by staying at Inverey, where, however, accommodation is spartan and strictly limited. As I have already said, Lochnagar may be climbed from Braemar and also from Crathie, but neither of these approaches is so fascinating as that from Ballater which includes the walk along Glen Muick, one of the wildest valleys in the district.

On the western side, Aviemore is relatively nearer the range and well placed for the ascents of Cairn Gorm, Cairn Lochan, Braeriach, and Sgoran Dubh. It is now possible to motor all the way to Glenmore Lodge from which the two former hills are usually climbed. But this form of transport is useless beyond Coylum Bridge for approaching the latter unless the climber is prepared to risk being bogged by taking his vehicle as far as the entrance to Gleann Einich. Here

A Camera in the Cairngorms

there is a place, high above the stream, where a small car may be turned round but beyond this point it is even painful to use a bicycle. The road as far as the Upper Bothy, now in ruins, is the worst I have ever encountered anywhere in the British hills: in some places it is impossible to advance except on foot.

The two centres on the eastern flanks of the Cairngorms are easily reached by rail and bus, or by bus alone from Aberdeen; and, of course, Aviemore is an important station on the L.M.S. main line between Perth and Inverness. Since, however, many tourists prefer to approach the district on foot, or to vary the route by car, I have included the following notes on alternatives, some of which take advantage of the Mounth roads crossing the range from south to north. Three of them are important ways across the Grampians—the Slug road from Stonehaven to Banchory, the Cairn o' Mount from Fettercairn to the same terminus, and the Cairnwell, which passes the Spittal of Glenshee between Blairgowie and Braemar. The rest of them are hill tracks, still occasionally employed for driving sheep, but largely disused. They are undisputed rights of way, and, avoiding the dips in the ridges, traverse the broad tops where the absence of large areas of boggy ground provide better walking.

1. Rail to Stonehaven, walk over the Slug Road to Banchory and then train or bus to Ballater.
2. Rail to Brechin and Edzell, walk to Fettercairn and thence over the Cairn o' Mount to Banchory.
3. Rail to Edzell, walk up Glen Esk to Tarfside, thence over the Fungle Road to Aboyne and on to Ballater by rail.
4. Rail to Kirriemuir, ride to Milton of Clova and walk over the Capel Mounth to Loch Muick, thence to Ballater.
5. Follow the same route to the commencement of the Capel Mounth but keep to the left to Bachnagairn, thence traverse Sandy Hillock to Loch Muick.
6. Follow Route 5, but go left through Glen Doll and keep to the Jocks Road over Tolmount, descending to Loch Callater for Braemar.
7. Rail to Blairgowie and motor through Glen Shee over the Devil's Elbow and descend by the Cairnwell to Braemar.
8. Rail to Blair Atholl and walk through Glen Tilt to White Bridge, thence via the Linn of Dee to Inverey and Braemar.
9. Rail to Kingussie, motor to Drumguish, and walk over the moors into Glen Feshie whence attain the Geldie Burn and descend to White Bridge for Braemar.
10. Rail to Kincraig, motor to Feshiebridge, whence join Route 9.
11. Rail to Aviemore, ride to Coylum Bridge, and walk through the Lairig Ghru.
12. Rail to Nethybridge and go through the Lairig an Laoigh to Derry Lodge.

Introductory Notes

13. Rail to Nethybridge and ride to Tomintoul, whence walk by way of Loch Builg to Braemar or go through Glen Gairn to Ballater.

As will be observed, many of these routes involve upwards of 30 miles of hard walking so that the pedestrian must be prepared to sleep out in one of the remote bothies or disused lodges, if bad weather makes their completion impossible in the day.

ACCOMMODATION

In normal times it is not always easy to find suitable accommodation at hotels and farms in the British Hills, and in the high season the problem is aggravated by the large influx of visitors who take their holidays during July and August. The position could be alleviated, to some extent, by the staggering of holidays and it may not be long before an attempt is made to bring this about. At present, however, it is difficult enough to book a room for a specified period, let alone to obtain one on chance, even by personal application; and these conditions appertain in districts such as the English Lakes and the Central Highlands, where accommodation is not inadequate because it has been progressively increased as the neighbourhoods have grown in popularity.

Unhappily this state of affairs cannot be said to exist in the Cairngorms and, after making inquiries and observations on the spot, I have come to the conclusion that it is worse off in this respect than any other mountain district in the country. The situation is made still more trying by the fact that existing habitations are at such vast distances from the popular climbs; which means that every walk into the heart of these hills is raised almost to the level of an expedition of some magnitude. It may well be that the great landowners and others having shooting, fishing, and deer-stalking interests, would not wish the position to be otherwise, but as it is probable the district will become one of our great National Parks where our post-war youth will be encouraged to take healthy exercise, find freedom, and learn to appreciate the beauties of Nature, drastic means will have to be taken to remedy the defect. This could be done by the acquisition of shooting-lodges or by the erection of hostels in the remote glens. But if the latter course was found to be the only solution, buildings must be constructed of materials toning in unobtrusively with the landscape.

The advantages of such a scheme would be tremendous because it would immediately solve the problem of the tramper. He generally is the youth who wishes to climb the most interesting peaks and to see the best things the district has to offer. But to accomplish this in a short holiday he must sleep in different places *en route* to save going over the same approaches again and again. Thus, he would enter the district at one point and leave it at another, spending a few days here and there near the scenes of his exploits. If he happened to be an indoor worker, he might get off the train looking anything but fit, and after a fortnight's strenuous walking with his belongings in his rucksack, would return to his job in robust health, already planning to repeat this performance in some other equally delectable place during the following year.

This sort of holiday is inexpensive and within the reach of all, if cheap and adequate accommodation is there to facilitate it. Imagine the establishment of such a chain of hostels in the Cairngorms which would make it possible for anyone to complete the following tour starting from Kirriemuir:

1. Walk up Glen Clova, cross the Mounth Road and drop down to Loch Muick to sleep at Hostel No. 1.
2. Spend the day exploring the Dubh Loch and return by traversing the Broad Cairn.
3. Climb Lochnagar, walk round the crest of the corrie, and descend by Loch Callater to Braemar to sleep at Hostel No. 2.
4. Spend the day exploring Deeside as far as the Chest of Dee.
5. Walk down to Invercauld Bridge and then traverse Gleann an t'Slugain to Loch Builg to sleep at Hostel No. 3.
6. Climb Ben Avon, go over the Sneck, and traverse Beinn a'Bhuird on the way to Glen Derry to sleep at Hostel No. 4.
7. Spend the day climbing Ben Macdhui to take in Loch Avon.
8. Walk through the Lairig Ghru as far as the foot of Castle Hill to sleep at Hostel No. 5.
9. Climb Carn Eilrig and walk up to Braeriach, then traverse the plateau to Cairn Toul and descend to Loch Einich to sleep at Hostel No. 6.
10. Spend the day making the circuit of the Loch by the high-level route to take in Sgoran Dubh.
11. Walk through Gleann Einich to Coylum Bridge to sleep at Hostel No. 7.
12. Walk through the Forest of Glen More by Loch Morlich to the foot of Ryvoan to sleep at Hostel No. 8.
13. Climb Cairn Gorm, traverse the ridge over Cairn Lochan to the Lurcher's Crag, and descend through Rothiemurchus to sleep again at either Hostel No. 5 or 7.
14. Walk by way of Loch an Eilein to Aviemore to catch the train home.

This comprehensive fortnight's tour, embracing the best scenery in the district, could of course be varied to suit individual tastes. But to widen its scope hostels would be necessary in Glen Feshie and at several points on Speyside. If the scheme I have been bold enough to adumbrate were modelled on these lines, it would be an immediate success. Its smooth working would depend in no small degree upon the wayfarer having every consideration for the landowners, especially during the shooting season, although it is doubtful if the new era of taxation will ever permit this exclusive sport to return to its former favour. Having enlarged upon this scheme in detail, it now only remains for those in a position to do so, to make a grateful gesture to our youth either by presenting some of their lodges to the nation, or else

Introductory Notes

by placing at its disposal the sites for the erection of the necessary hostels. Such a move, I feel sure, would be received by the public with acclamation.

When I go on these mountaineering expeditions it is always a matter of some concern to my friends whether I shall find suitable lodgings, because I never book accommodation throughout in advance. This seems a good opportunity for setting their minds at rest, so I will give an account of my experiences on the present trip since it covers such difficult country.

The reason for my apparent lack of detailed planning will be clear after a perusal of these notes, but I will say at the outset that I always reserve a room beforehand at the first port of call; but only because my future movements are controlled entirely by the weather. Now, successful landscape photography depends in the first place upon favourable lighting which occurs only under good atmospheric conditions, and this means the exercise of much patience during the dull and rainy periods, if camera studies are to be secured worthy of inclusion in this series of books. I never rely upon chance shots although I occasionally get them but, instead, plan each route in advance so that I can take advantage of the lighting in relation to the topography of the country. It will, therefore, be obvious that if I booked accommodation on pre-arranged dates, I might stay too long in one place while the weather was good and too short a time in another while it was bad.

On the present occasion I reserved a room at the Loriston Hotel in Ballater, the only place here where accommodation could be obtained. On arrival I soon discovered that difficulties would arise once I contemplated a move to Braemar because none of the hotels were open and war-time problems made it difficult to secure rooms in the village. I had two good friends in Aberdeen who were anxious that my trip should be a success—Mrs. Bruce and Mrs. Hendry—both wives of eminent medical men. The former is a sister of my friend Scottie Legge, who, by the way, is one of those first-class golfers who have migrated south of the border in search of a more congenial climate, and who is, incidentally, a well-known raconteur of those subtle stories so much enjoyed by the members of the Walton Heath Golf Club! These ladies knew the difficulties I should encounter and they were kind enough to suggest places where I might find accommodation in Braemar. I was fortunate in one of their recommendations, for Miss MacHardy, of "Mayfield," came to my rescue and could not do enough to make my sojourn in her house comfortable. In fact, she displayed that kindness and consideration which is typical of Scottish hospitality at its best. When I crossed over to Speyside I stayed first at "The Dell" in Rothiemurchus, well placed for easy access to Coylum Bridge and beyond. I then moved over to the Cairngorm Hotel in Aviemore, which is the epitome of good food, excellent service, and first-class accommodation. In conclusion I must also pay tribute to the kindness of Mr. and Mrs. R. Thomson, who entertained me royally for a week-end in Elgin, a part of Scotland which I had not previously visited. Both these Scots are great lovers of the hills and especially of the Cairngorms.

GLEN MUICK

Glen Muick runs in a south-westerly direction from Ballater to Loch Muick where it bends to the west and ends in the deep recesses of the White Mounth. A public road extends for some eight miles along the south side of the glen and terminates at the Spittal of Glen Muick, an ancient hospice now used as a farm. The road surface is reasonably good as far as the Linn of Muick, but beyond that point it is rough and stony, being more suitable for a shooting-brake than for an ordinary low-slung car. A sandy cart track continues to Lochend, a small lodge situated near the outflow of the lake, where the Capel Mounth track rises to the left across the moor to give access to Glen Clova. The main path keeps high above the southern shore of the loch and again bifurcates at the Black Burn, the left branch zigzagging over the hills to Bachnagairn, whilst the right branch follows the lakeside and gradually falls to its sandy head. Here it rises again in the direction of the Broad Cairn to which it affords an easy ascent. A rather indistinct track goes through the heather round the head of Loch Muick to a footbridge over the river coming down from the Dubh Loch, but the main stream has been diverted and can only be crossed by fording its deep stony bed.

On the north shore of the loch and half a mile from its head stands the Glas-allt Shiel, a small lodge on a delta built for Queen Victoria in 1869. The site is both wild and remote, but the sheltering plantation of conifers imparts a softness to the landscape otherwise barren in the extreme. The lodge is connected with the distant highway by a private road threading the northern slopes of the glen, but to the west a stony track strikes uphill, and, keeping well above the Allt an Dubh Loch, rises some 800 ft. in two miles to end at this gloomy tarn set in an amphitheatre of precipitous, forbidding cliffs. The Dubh Loch is 13 miles from Ballater and 1,433 ft. above it, but 653 ft. is accounted for in the run up to Loch Muick.

I cycled up Glen Muick on three occasions, twice to the loch and once to the foot of Lochnagar whose ascent is described later. I passed through the beautiful band of birches crowding the entrance to the glen and then emerged upon a scene of desolation, for the once lovely woods to the south of the road had been recently felled and the tree-stumps imparted a melancholy note. As I approached the narrow part of the valley, I espied two beautiful larches away up the hillside and I could not resist climbing up to them because they made such a graceful foreground to the white top of Morven (3). The road keeps to the very edge of the deep ravine, and as I approached the Linn of Muick the music of its fall grew louder and more tuneful (2). Beyond it the wild and desolate moorland stretches away to the west where its background is characterised by the steep slopes enclosing Loch Muick. The rough road continues to rise for some distance, and as this was my first long

2. THE LINN OF MUICK

ride on a bicycle, I began to grow saddle weary! However, I soon forgot this discomfort when the summit of the White Mounth appeared above the intervening foothills on my right. First came the small cone of the Little Pap, then the massive rounded top of Cuidhe Crom, followed by the cliffs of Lochnagar peeping over the dip which swept up to the graceful cone of the Meikle Pap on the extreme right (4). I pushed on past the Spittal of Glen Muick and descended the last half-mile of road to leave my bicycle at Lochend.

I walked along the rising path above the loch and from the first footbridge looked back to its sandy beach enclosed by the foothills of the White Mounth (5). The lake occupies the floor of a gigantic trough whose slopes are precipitous and littered with scree. There were moments when the scene reminded me of the grander Wastwater in distant English Lakeland, for it is presided over by the smooth cone of the Broad Cairn bearing some resemblance to Great Gable, although its lines are scarcely as graceful (6). I continued along this revealing terrace walk, but as I had only left my hotel after lunch, I retraced my steps on reaching the Black Burn. I picked up my bicycle and the subsequent bumpy ride downhill brought me back to Ballater in an hour.

On the second occasion I allowed a day for the trip with the hope of reaching the Dubh Loch. The weather, however, let me down, for on reaching the stream descending from the tarn, the storm clouds gathered and it began to rain. I took what shelter I could find but, as conditions rapidly deteriorated, I retreated and cycled back to Ballater wet to the skin.

4. LOCHNAGAR FROM THE SPITTAL OF GLEN MUICK

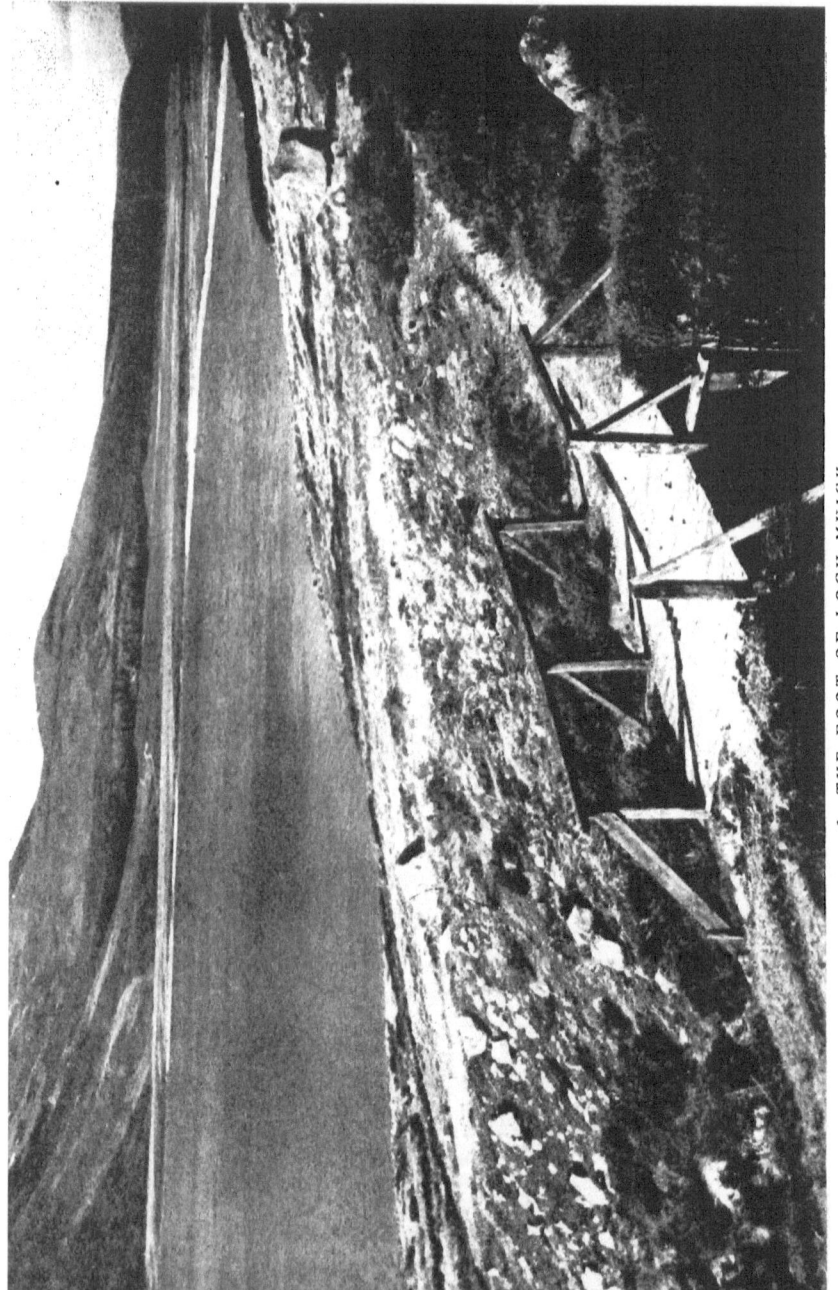
5. THE FOOT OF LOCH MUICK

6. LOOKING WEST TO THE BROAD CAIRN AND THE HEAD OF LOCH MUICK

LOCHNAGAR

In the spring the wayfarer travelling westwards from Aberdeen may catch a glimpse of the great snow-covered summit of Lochnagar before he reaches Ballater. But if he wishes to obtain a clearer view he must make for the bridge over the Dee where the vast plateau of the White Mounth will be seen rising above the nearer and more shapely Coyles of Muick. If he goes along Deeside he will notice the group from time to time, and not the least interesting of these prospects is obtained from the low hills to the north of Balmoral, whilst at Invercauld Bridge, farther to the west, the mountain with its small conical summit is a conspicuous feature.

Lochnagar dominates the Royal Forest of Balmoral and although its highest top is only 3,786 ft. above sea level, and the thirty-third in order of altitude in the Highlands, the shapeliness of its foothills, combined with the superb crescent of cliffs forming its eastern corrie, raise it to an incomparable place in all the mountain scenes in the country. Its precipices consist of coarse red granite which weathers both horizontally and vertically, and these lines of weakness impart to the cliffs an illusion of gigantic masonry. In course of time the upper blocks become dangerously undercut and ultimately fall to the floor of the corrie some 1,200 ft. below. They are thus a risky venue for the rock climber, but the mountaineer who revels in sensational snow ascents will find in the prodigious gully known as the Black Spout something to satisfy his tastes. The ascent of the mountain presents no dangers or difficulties if the eastern corrie is avoided; and it is a common occurrence for small boys to climb it, under the guidance of someone familiar with the various routes. It is scarcely necessary to point out that novices should be kept well away from the snow cornices on the upper plateau owing to their unknown dimensions. The summit of Lochnagar is some 14 miles from Ballater and about 5 miles from the Spittal of Glen Muick, so that even if transport to its base is available, the ascent requires a full day for the complete enjoyment of all the majestic scenes.

When I arrived in Ballater, a glittering white mantle cloaked the summit and well down to the base of the Meikle Pap. Unhappily, on the first evening, a change in the direction of the wind brought rain which did not cease for four days. This precipitation, combined with a rise in temperature, melted much of the snow so that, when I climbed it, the patchy snowfields detracted considerably from the scintillating beauty which usually characterises it in the brilliant spring sunshine. I obtained permission from the King's Factor to cycle along the private road on the north side of Glen Muick, and in just under two hours of uphill pedalling against a westerly wind, I reached Allt-na-Guibhsaich where I left my machine under the trees. The day was warm and sunny but dulled by much cirrus which stretched across the whole sky. I followed the well-defined path through the plantation of

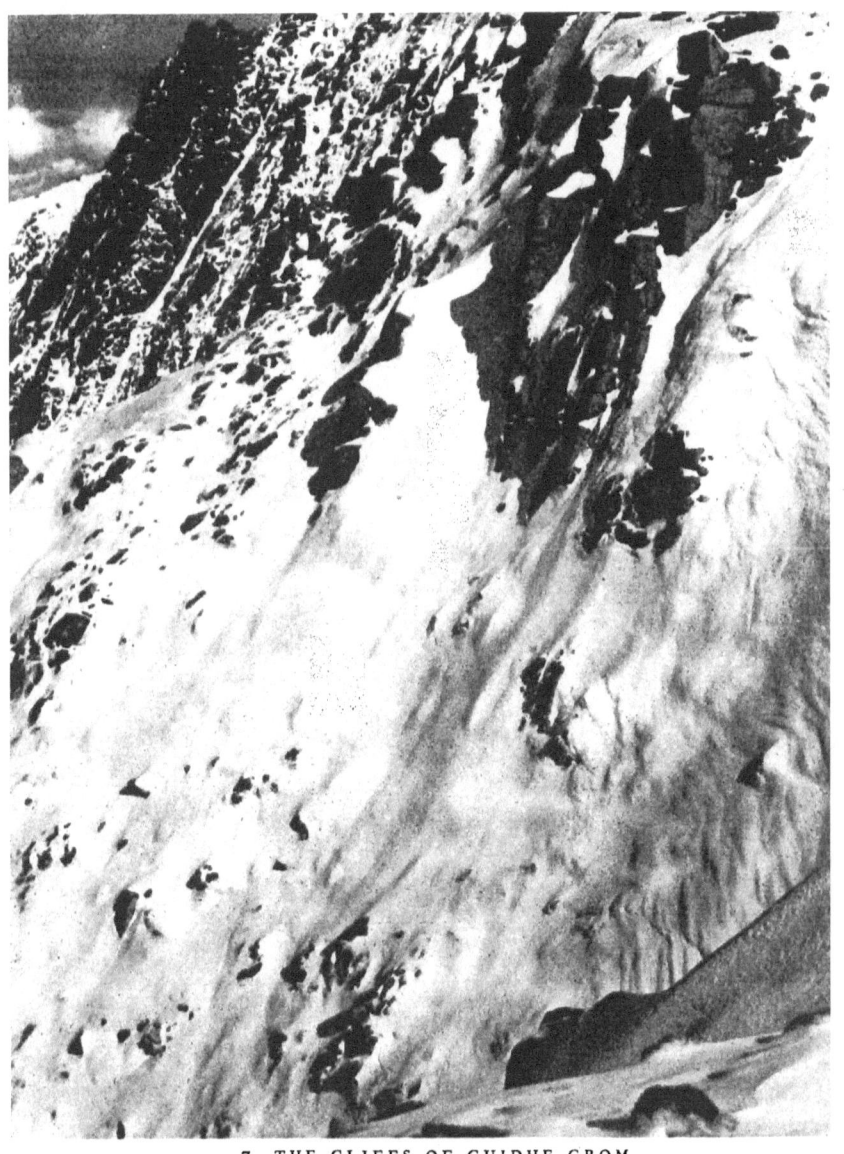
7. THE CLIFFS OF CUIDHE CROM

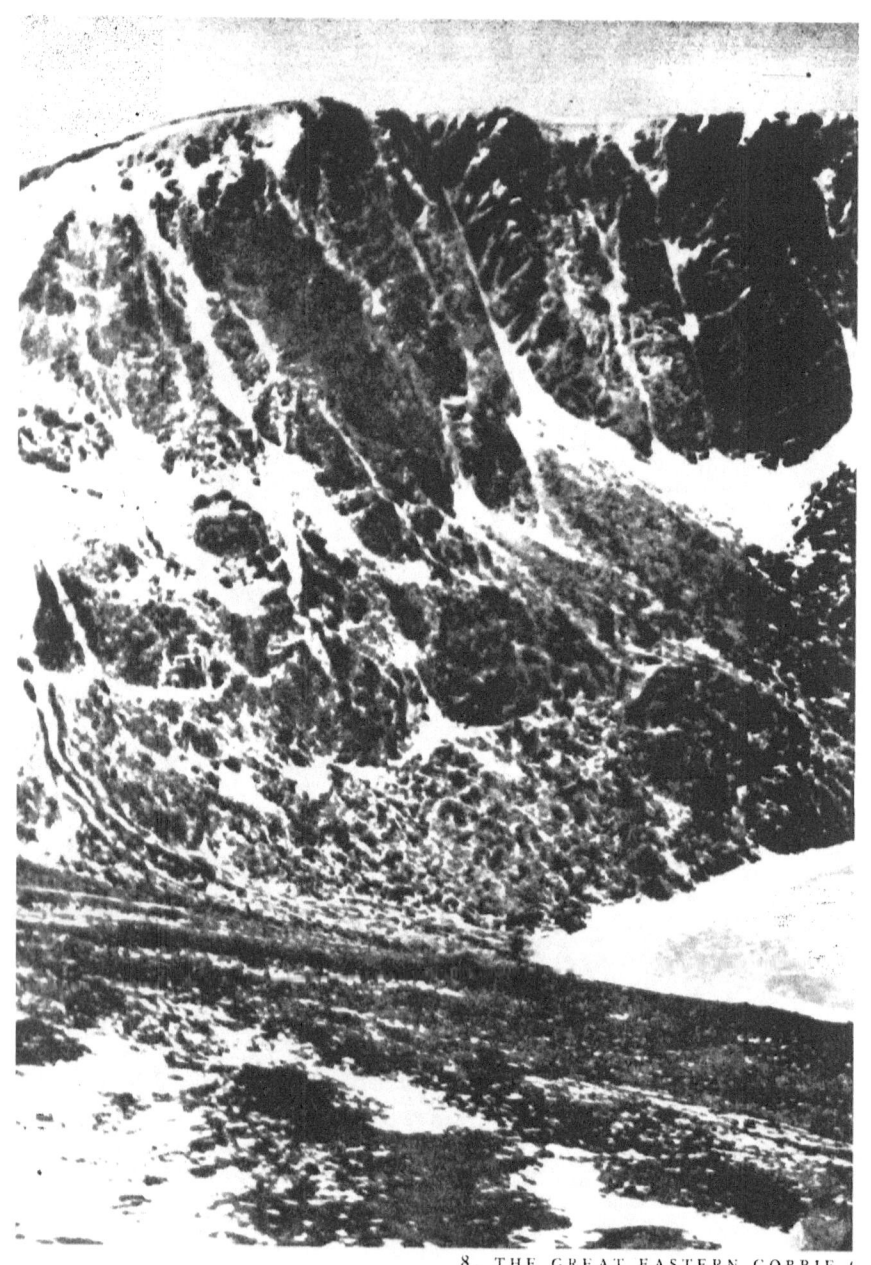

8. THE GREAT EASTERN CORRIE
The summit of the mountain   Cac

LOCHNAGAR FROM THE MEIKLE PAP
Lochnagar is on the extreme right of the skyline

Lochnagar

conifers and on emerging on the open moorland, kept to the track high above the left bank of the stream. In less than an hour I had rounded the shoulder of Conachcraig and was standing on the small col, which, at a height of 2,291 ft., joins this outlier with the main group. From this vantage point the cone of the Meikle Pap towered overhead and to its right the snow-clad summits of Beinn a'Bhuird and Ben Avon made a fine but distant background to the north. The track is confusing here because it drops on the far side of the ridge and then branches to the left for the Meikle Pap. Thereafter it is clear enough and at a height of 2,800 ft. I encountered the Foxes' Well, marked by a small cairn and affording the last drink on this ascent. To the south rises the steep zigzag known as the "Ladder," which gives direct access to the Cuidhe Crom. But I made for the col on its right and, as I climbed, the precipices engirdling the corrie gradually came into view. Here I searched for a viewpoint which would display these magnificent cliffs to advantage with the frozen lochan at their base. I had, however, to ascend the Meikle Pap to find one that satisfied me (8). The light was not too good owing to the rather dense cirrus, but in the far north this canopy was being replaced by fine cumulus. The slow transformation of the heavens, however, took too long to reach the dome above Lochnagar, so I returned to the col and climbed along the edge of the precipices on to Cuidhe Crom (7).

The sun had gained in power by the time I reached this belvedere and the more westerly viewpoint permitted a full-length prospect of the Black Spout to the north across the void. The snow was melting fast and every hollow on the summit plateau now held water. I advanced along the edge of the cliffs, and, after passing the Red Spout (9), scaled the final slopes which led to the vertical precipices engirdling the grandest part of the corrie (10). By this time the light was superb with fine cumulus drifting across a purple sky and I carefully probed the snow with my ice-axe as I walked out on to the point of each of the airy buttresses (11). The conical top of Cac Carn Beag now became a prominent feature across the lip of the corrie, with a glimpse of the upper section of the Black Spout immediately below (12). I circled the great cornice overhanging this gigantic gully, on either side of which the terrific cliffs disappeared into the abyss far below (13). It was now only a short step across the intervening snowfield to the summit of the mountain (14) where I examined the Cairngorm Club Indicator erected in July 1924, and in the brilliantly clear atmosphere was able to pick out the distant summit of Ben Nevis on the western horizon (15). Scanning the encircling hills, I noticed the corrie dominated by the Stuic, a fine buttress above Loch nan Eun (16).

I left the summit of Lochnagar regretfully at 3.30 p.m. and walked over to its subsidiary top, Cac Carn Mor, only 18 ft. below and the point at which the Braemar track descends to the west (17). The return journey along the edge of the precipices was an enchanting experience (18), and I soon had before me the whole shattered face of Cuidhe Crom (19). I traversed this quickly and, descending the "Ladder," collected my bicycle at 5.45 p.m.

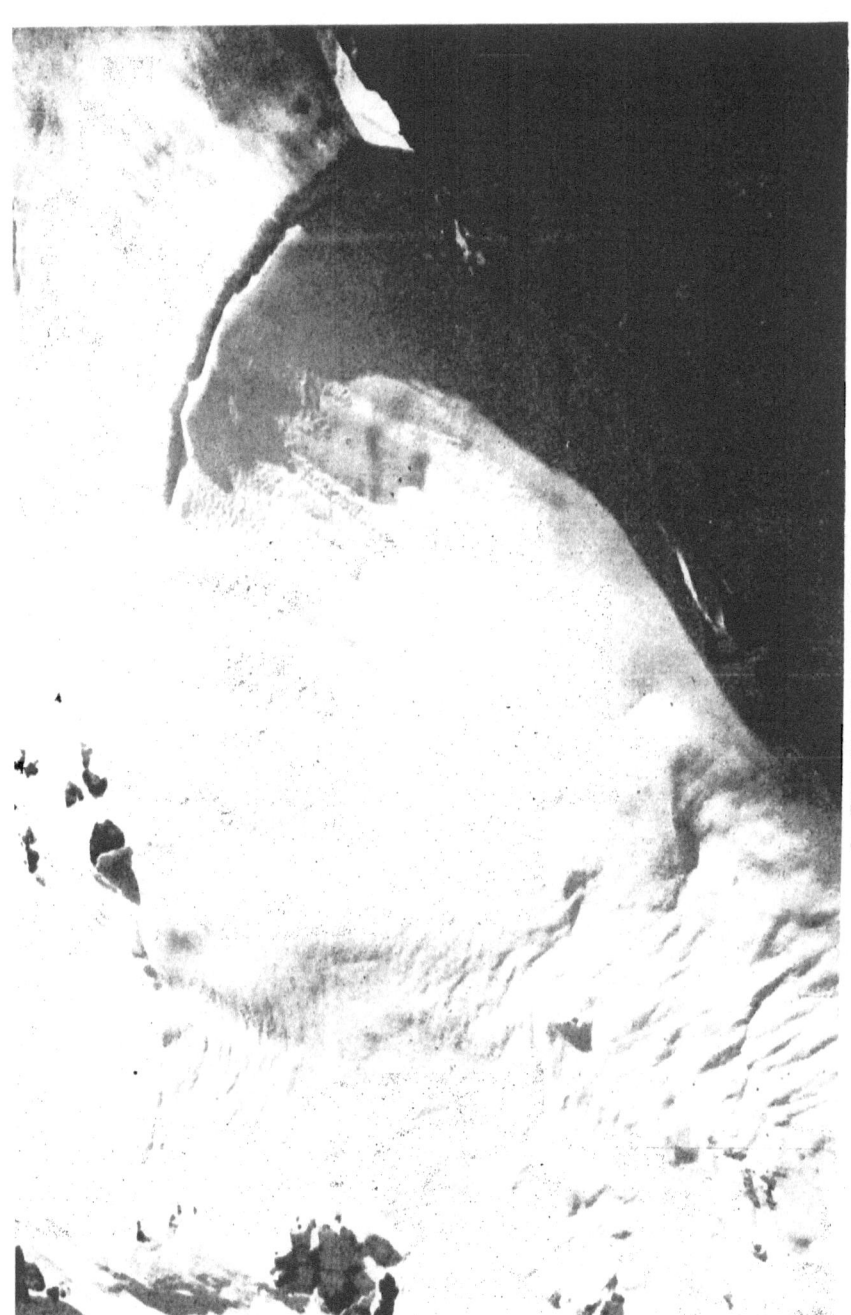

9. THE EXIT OF RED SPOUT

10. THE LAST RISE TO THE SUMMIT PLATEAU

11. THE PRECIPICES OF LOCHNAGAR

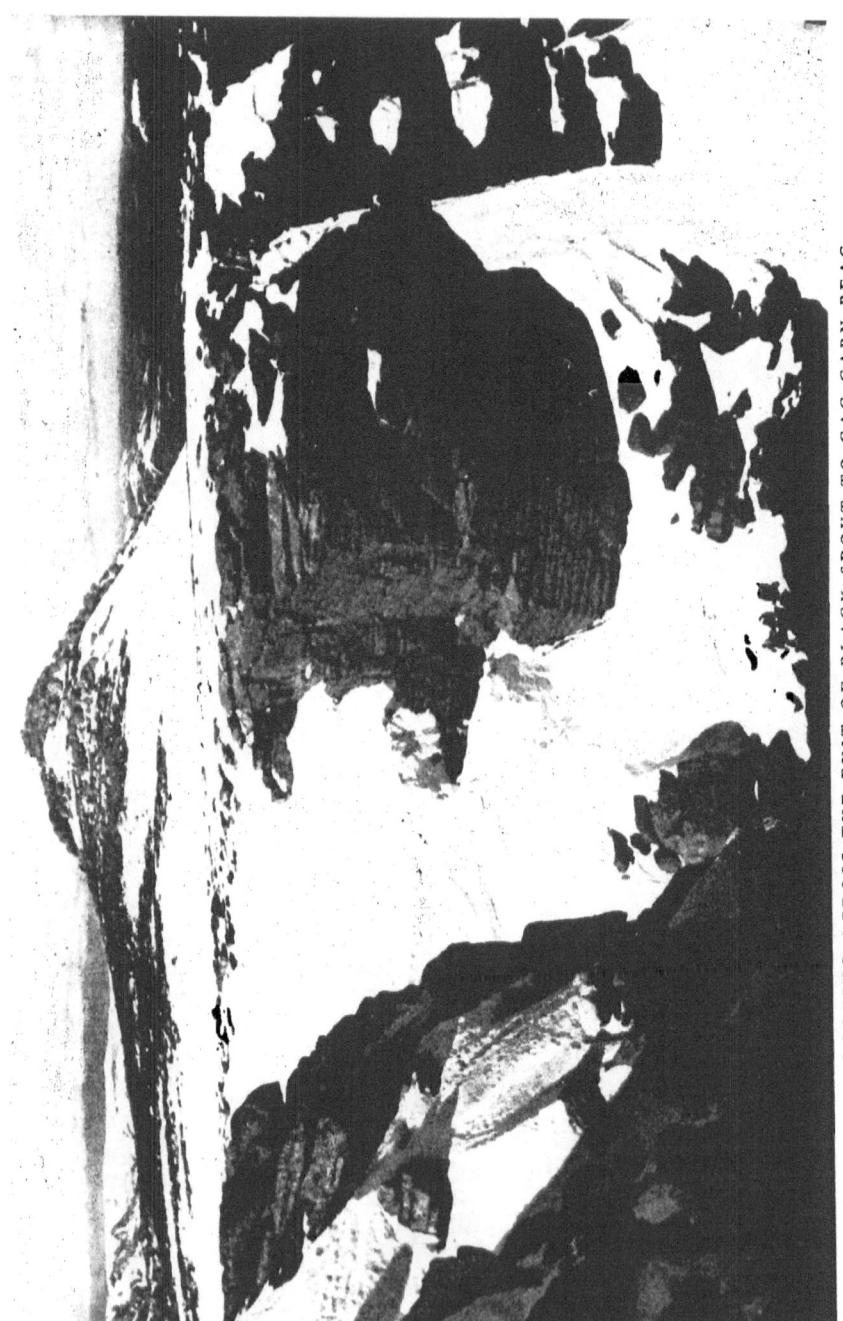

12. LOOKING ACROSS THE EXIT OF BLACK SPOUT TO CAC CARN BEAG

13. THE EASTERN PROSPECT FROM THE BLACK SPOUT

14. THE SUMMIT OF LOCHNAGAR (3,786 feet)

15. THE INDICATOR ON LOCHNAGAR

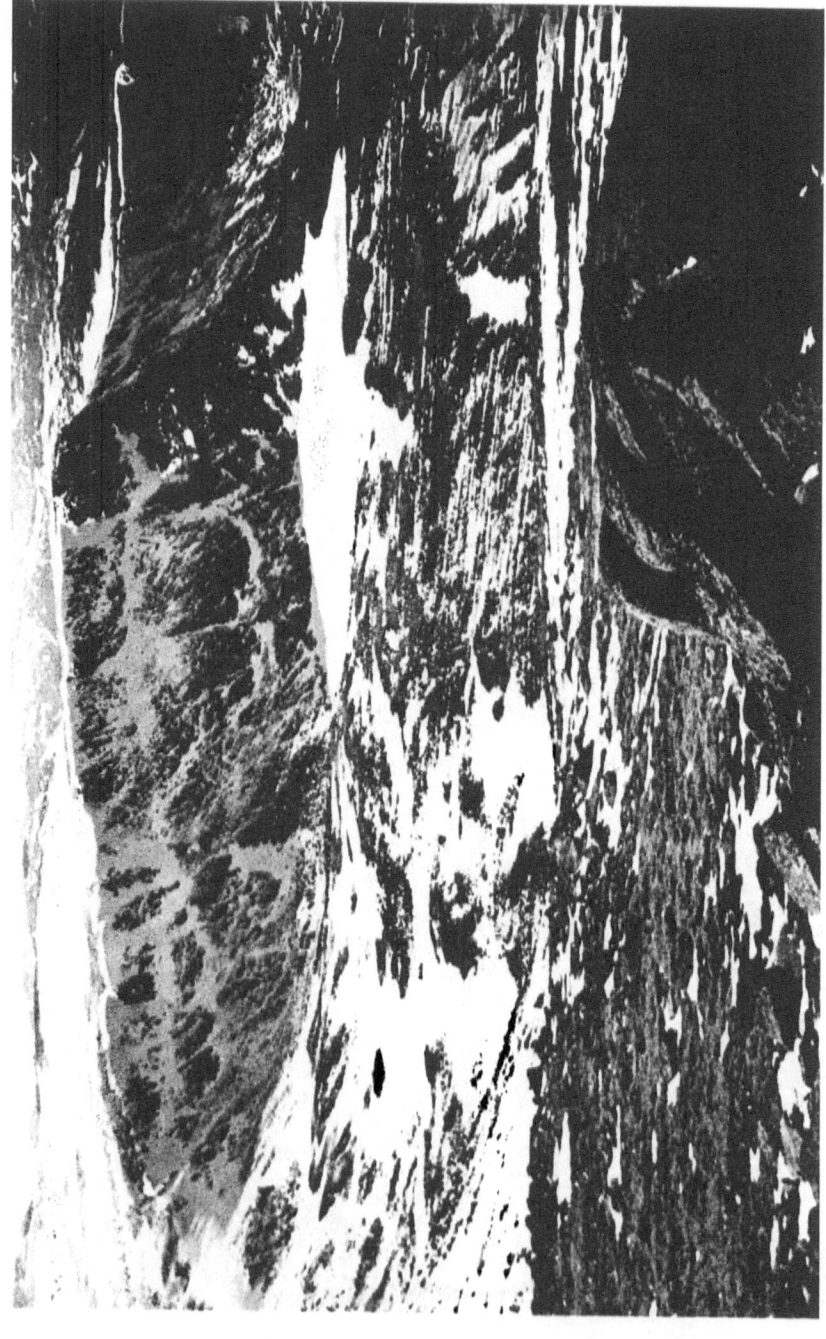

17. CAC CARN MOR (3,768 feet)

18. SNOW CORNICES ON THE SUMMIT PLATEAU

19. CUIDHE CROM FROM THE SUMMIT PLATEAU

DEESIDE

The River Dee is 85 miles long and passes through some of the most magnificent and varied scenery in Scotland. It rises at a height of 4,000 ft. on the vast plateau to the south of the summit of Braeriach, and no other river in Britain has such an elevated source. Known as the Wells of Dee, it gathers strength from other tributaries on this high ground and then plunges over the edge of the corrie to fall some 500 ft. as a foaming cascade. Here it flows through the bed of An Garbh Coire, and on reaching the Lairig Ghru is joined by the stream coming down from the Pools of Dee some 2 miles to the north. The innumerable burns feeding it rapidly increase its volume, and by the time it reaches the Devil's Point it has become a powerful river. Flowing in a southerly direction, the Dee bends to the east at the Chest of Dee and below White Bridge is joined by the Geldie Burn. So far the stream has threaded one of the wildest and most desolate regions in the Cairngorms, but at the Linn of Dee a transformation takes place, for thereafter it wends its way through some of the most beautifully wooded stretches in the country. Passing Mar Lodge, Braemar, Invercauld House, and the famous Balmoral Castle, it reaches Ballater, whence it flows through Aboyne and Banchory before falling into the North Sea at Aberdeen.

There are so many beauty spots on Deeside that it is impossible to mention them all. As I have said elsewhere, I always prefer to walk or ride upstream, for then the waterplay is more fascinating and provides many a scene which would otherwise escape notice. Even at Ballater the Dee has attained considerable proportions and is spanned by a bridge which has been rebuilt on several occasions (22). Magnificent Scots Pine (23) fringe its banks all the way up to the Old Bridge of Dee at Invercauld, one of the river's most lovely settings with the great mass of Lochnagar forming a splendid background (21), and the rough road leading to the Falls of Garbh Allt in Ballochbuie Forest presenting a typical Scottish landscape (24). To the west the trees are less prolific which permits a prospect of the great corries of Beinn a'Bhuird on the distant horizon (25). Hereabouts is Invercauld House in a delightful setting on the northern banks of the river (26), and some two miles farther on is Braemar Castle (27). The glen widens above Braemar where the Dee flows in graceful bends amid sterner surroundings and beyond Victoria Bridge passes below Inverey, the last hamlet on Deeside (28). Two miles above, it rushes through the narrow rocky ravine at the Linn of Dee where the road is carried over it by a sturdily built bridge (20), beyond which it sweeps along through the fastnesses of the hills as a sparkling and lively torrent (29).

20. THE LINN OF DEE

21. LOCHNAGAR FROM THE O

IDGE OF DEE AT INVERCAULD

22. THE DEE AT BALLATER

23. THE WHITE MOUNTH FROM THE DEE

25. THE CORRIES OF BEINN A'BHUIRD FROM THE DEE AT INVERCAULD

26. EVENING AT INVERCAULD HOUSE

27. BRAEMAR CASTLE

28. INVEREY

29. LOOKING WEST FROM THE LINN OF DEE

BEN MACDHUI

Ben Macdhui (4,296 ft.) is the highest mountain in the Cairngorms, and together with its outlier Cairn Gorm (4,084 ft.), forms the massive group rising between the Lairig an Laoigh on the east and the Lairig Ghru on the west. The summit is scarcely well proportioned and consists of a flattish rounded top which perhaps presents its most graceful aspect when seen from Cairn Gorm. The two are connected by a broad high plateau which nowhere falls below the 3,600 ft. contour. The supporting slopes of Ben Macdhui are set at a gentle angle, excepting on the west, where they fall steeply to the Lairig Ghru. The ascent of the mountain, therefore, presents no difficulties whatever but vast distances have to be covered.

Two famous lochs lie in the heart of the group: Loch Avon at an altitude of 2,377 ft. and Loch Etchachan at 3,058 ft. The former is set deep in the hills amid one of the most impressive and sombre amphitheatres in the Highlands and is so remote that, were it not for the Shelter Stone where a night may be spent, it is doubtful if many climbers would ever see it. The latter, lying in more open ground, is of considerably less interest, and is passed in the usual ascent of Ben Macdhui.

As the crow flies the summit is actually nearer to Aviemore than Braemar, but unless its ascent is combined with that of Cairn Gorm, the expedition is lacking in interest. Those wishing to undertake it should drive to Glenmore Lodge, climb Cairn Gorm, and walk across the plateau to Ben Macdhui, descending by way of Creag an Leth-Choin and Rothiemurchus. The mountain, however, is more usually ascended from Braemar by way of Derry Lodge, beyond which there is a choice of two routes. The more popular of these is through Glen Derry and Coire Etchachan (total distance 7½ miles), but the more direct approach by Glen Luibeg and the fine ridge of Sron Riach is 2 miles shorter.

One of my objects in moving to Braemar was to climb Ben Macdhui under the most favourable conditions. I experienced two days of bad weather, but the third—Easter Monday—dawned with a cloudless sky, a brilliantly clear atmosphere, and a cold wind from the north-west. Two enthusiastic lovers of the hills, Dr. Ann Lindsay and Squadron-Leader McCullum, had arrived at Mayfield, and on being invited to accompany me they gladly accepted. We were lucky to get a lift as far as Black Bridge, two miles beyond the Linn of Dee, and although we had caught a glimpse of our objective from the vicinity of Inverey, we had a clear view of it with the cone of Derry Cairngorm on its right, as we started the two mile tramp to Derry Lodge (30). The invigorating atmosphere acted like wine and we swung along the rough road joyfully anticipating the long climb ahead. In half an hour we passed the empty shell of Derry Lodge (31), and as I had chosen the shorter route on account of the more favourable lighting, we crossed the

[*Continued on page 60*

30. BEN MACDHUI AND DERRY CAIRNGORM FROM BLACK BRIDGE

Ben Macdhui

wooden bridge over the Derry Burn, and passing the Keeper's Cottage at Luibeg, left the last habitation behind (32).

We followed the Lairig Ghru path for nearly two miles with Cairn a'Mhaim towering ahead of us, but on approaching it, took the track rising to the right. This mounts gently through the thick heather and, on rounding the slopes of the hill, we saw the ridge of Sron Riach to the north, its lines leading our eyes irresistibly aloft to the shapely snowy summit of Stob Coire Sputan Dearg (33). The limpid atmosphere induced us to under-estimate the distance of the peak and we had to do some hard climbing before attaining its summit. As we trudged steadily along the rising track, magnificent cumulus clouds were forming, and after crossing the Luibeg Burn we commenced the long ascent of Sron Riach. Patches of snow lay on the ridge but these did not interfere with our progress, and on reaching the 3,000 ft. contour we were rewarded by a superb view of Cairn Toul and its adjacent snow-filled corries beyond the long shadowed ridge of Cairn a'Mhaim to the west (34). Ahead of us Stob Coire Sputan Dearg rose into the sky, its snow mantle glittering in the brilliant sunshine. I left my companions and diverged to the right so that I could gaze upon this scene of Alpine splendour while ascending the crest of the ridge enclosing the corrie (35). Far below lay the frozen surface of the lonely Lochan Uaine, the second highest in the Cairngorms at an altitude of 3,142 ft. Whilst I climbed, the swish of miniature avalanches was the only sound to break the silence as they swept down the steep cliffs to come to rest on the surface of the loch. On nearing the summit I must have disturbed a Golden Eagle for one flew rapidly overhead and disappeared in the direction of Ben Macdhui. I was joined by my companions as I gained the red granite blocks on the top. About a mile to the west we could now perceive the flattish summit of Ben Macdhui, and after a short rest, turned our steps in this direction (36). It did not take us long to cross the intervening snowfield and we were soon sitting by the cairn (37). This mountain, like Lochnagar, has an indicator erected in 1925 by the Cairngorm Club, and we were able to identify many of the distant hills (38). While my companions were resting I wandered off to the west of the cairn in the direction of the Lairig Ghru so that I could more easily observe the long line of corries between Cairn Toul and Braeriach, one of the grandest prospects in the country. From this viewpoint the vastness of the An Garbh Coire became apparent with the sharp-pointed summit of Sgor an Lochan Uaine, known also as the Angel's Peak, rising steeply on its left and just behind Cairn Toul (39). The skyline swept round to the right to Braeriach which is supported by Coire Bhrochain and then fell away to Sron na Lairig and the lower tops to the north (40).

I returned to the cairn and we began the longer descent by way of Glen Derry. Recrossing the snowfield in the direction of Coire Sputan Dearg, we bore to the left along its line of northern cliffs and walked quickly down the gentle snow slopes stretching in an almost unbroken sweep down to Loch Etchachan. Here the snow round its frozen surface was more patchy and we could clearly see the great mass

31. DERRY LODGE

of Cairn Gorm through the depression beyond it (41). After passing the outflow of the loch, the deep trough of Coire Etchachan came into view with Glen Derry over 1,000 ft. below, backed by the great rounded plateau of Beinn a'Bhuird on the eastern horizon (42). We took advantage of some snow in the gullies to increase the pace of our descent, and after skirting the impressive cliffs of Creagan Etchachan, reached the Derry Burn where we looked back to admire the fine precipitous southern face of Beinn .Mheadhoin, a mountain characterised by the strange granite tors on its summit (43). At this point Glen Derry is barren and gloomy, but on gaining the track on its eastern slopes our attention was aroused by a herd of red deer, which on seeing us, rapidly disappeared in the direction of Derry Cairngorm. The tramp down the glen seemed endless and we were glad to pass the first gnarled pines heralding the approach of Derry Wood. Before being swallowed up by its gigantic trees, we cast one backward glance to the scene of our exploits (44). Derry Wood is one of the finest of ancient pine forest in Scotland and perhaps the most enchanting in the Cairngorms, but on this occasion we were far too tired to appreciate its beauty. On and on we went until the Lodge came into view, but on leaving it behind we were still faced with the tramp along the two miles of hard road to Black Bridge. We had arranged for a car to meet us here, and in what seemed a trice were whisked back to Braemar, so completing another grand day on the Hills.

The map distance of this circuit from Black Bridge is 17 miles, in addition to which I must have covered another three to secure these photographs. To this must also be added some six or seven thousand feet of ascent and descent which makes a fairly good day for one who has passed the fiftieth milestone. I think this circuit is perhaps more strenuous than that of Carn Mor Dearg and Ben Nevis, already described in my *Scotland through the Lens*. It is, of course, considerably longer although it does not involve so much climbing; at any rate I felt more fatigued on this occasion, but after a day's rest I was quite ready for another expedition.

22. CARN A'MHAIM FROM THE TRACK NEAR LUIBEG

33. SRON RIACH AND COIRE SPUTAN DEARG FROM GLEN LUIBEG

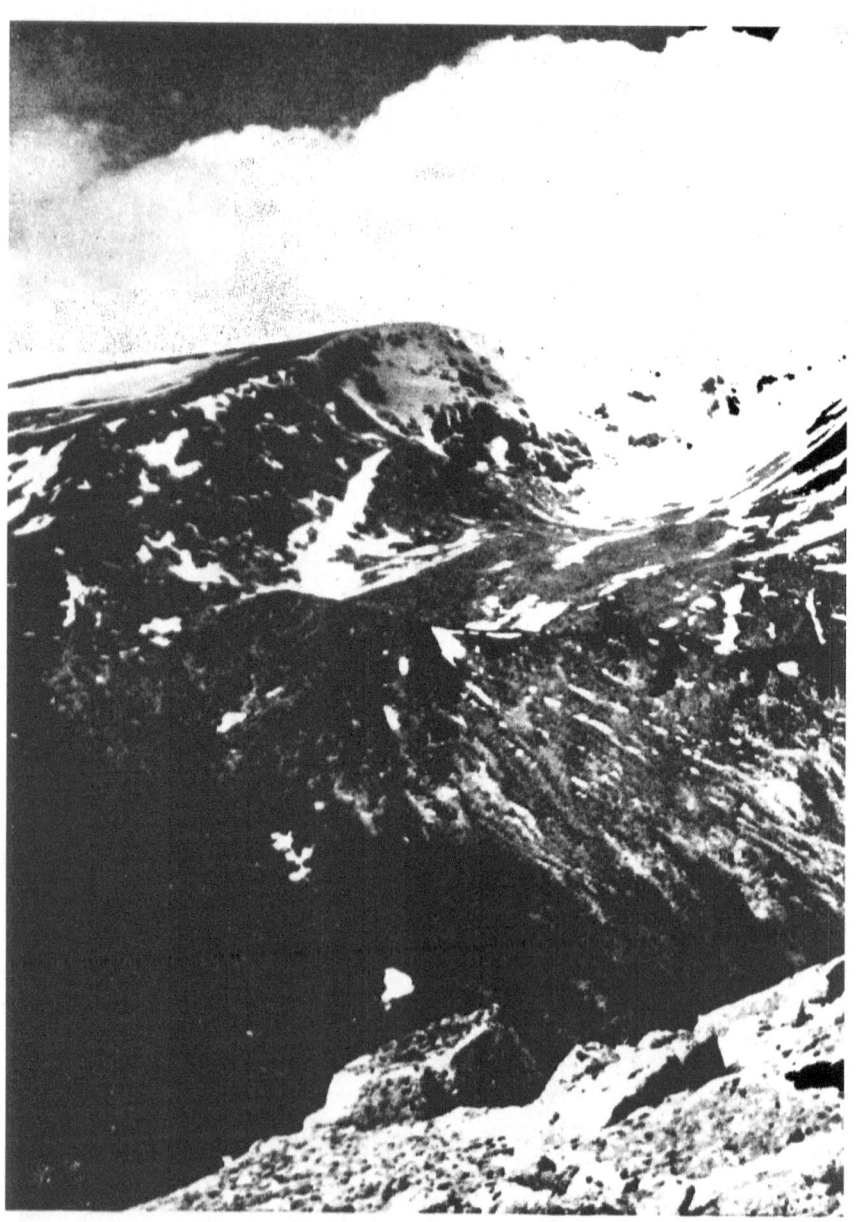

34. COIRE AN T'SAIGHDEIR A

CAIRN TOUL FROM SRON RIACH

35. STOB COIRE SPUTAN DEARG

36. CROSSING THE LAST SNOWFIELD

37. THE SUMMIT OF BEN MACDHUI (4,296 feet)

38. THE INDICATOR

39. AN GARBH CHOIRE FROM BEN MACDHUI

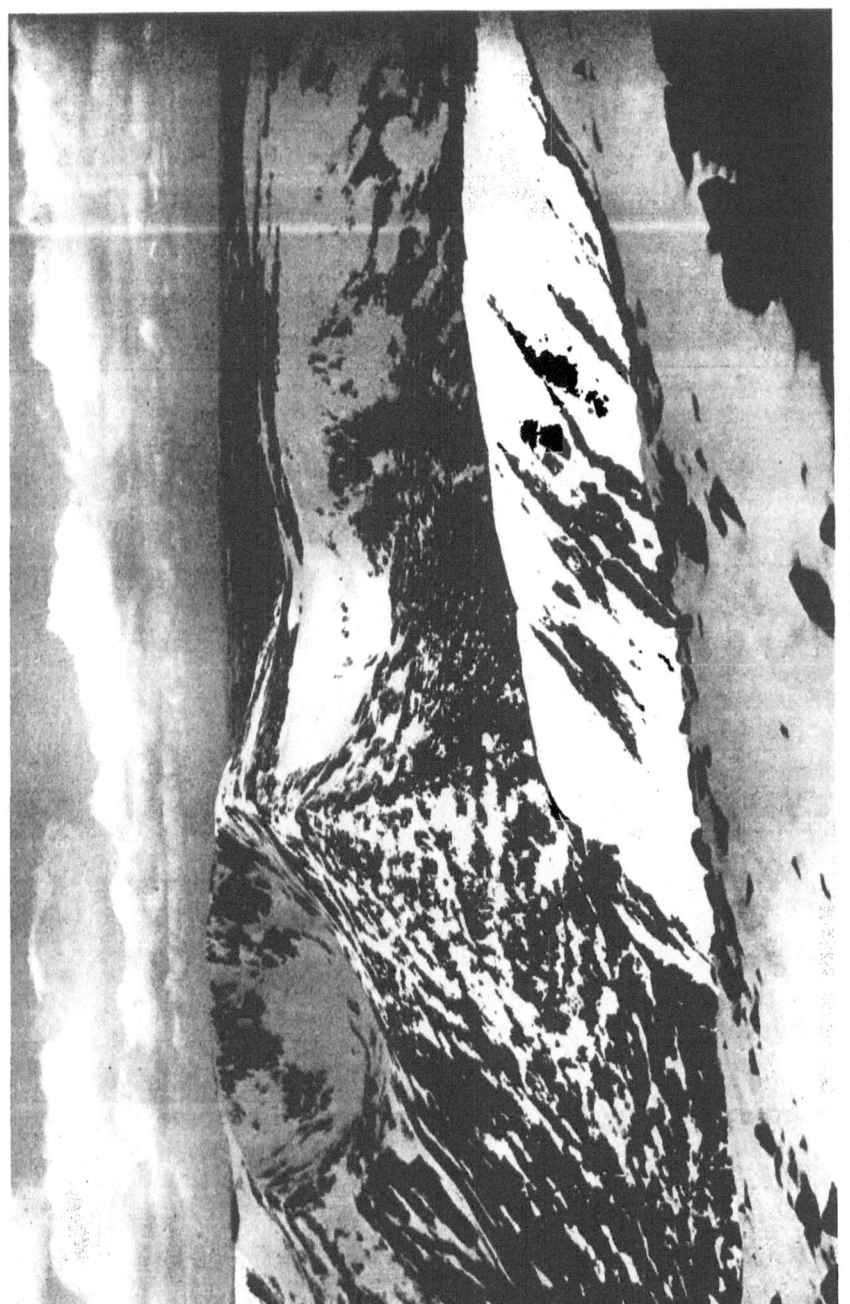

40. BRAERIACH AND COIRE BHROCHAIN

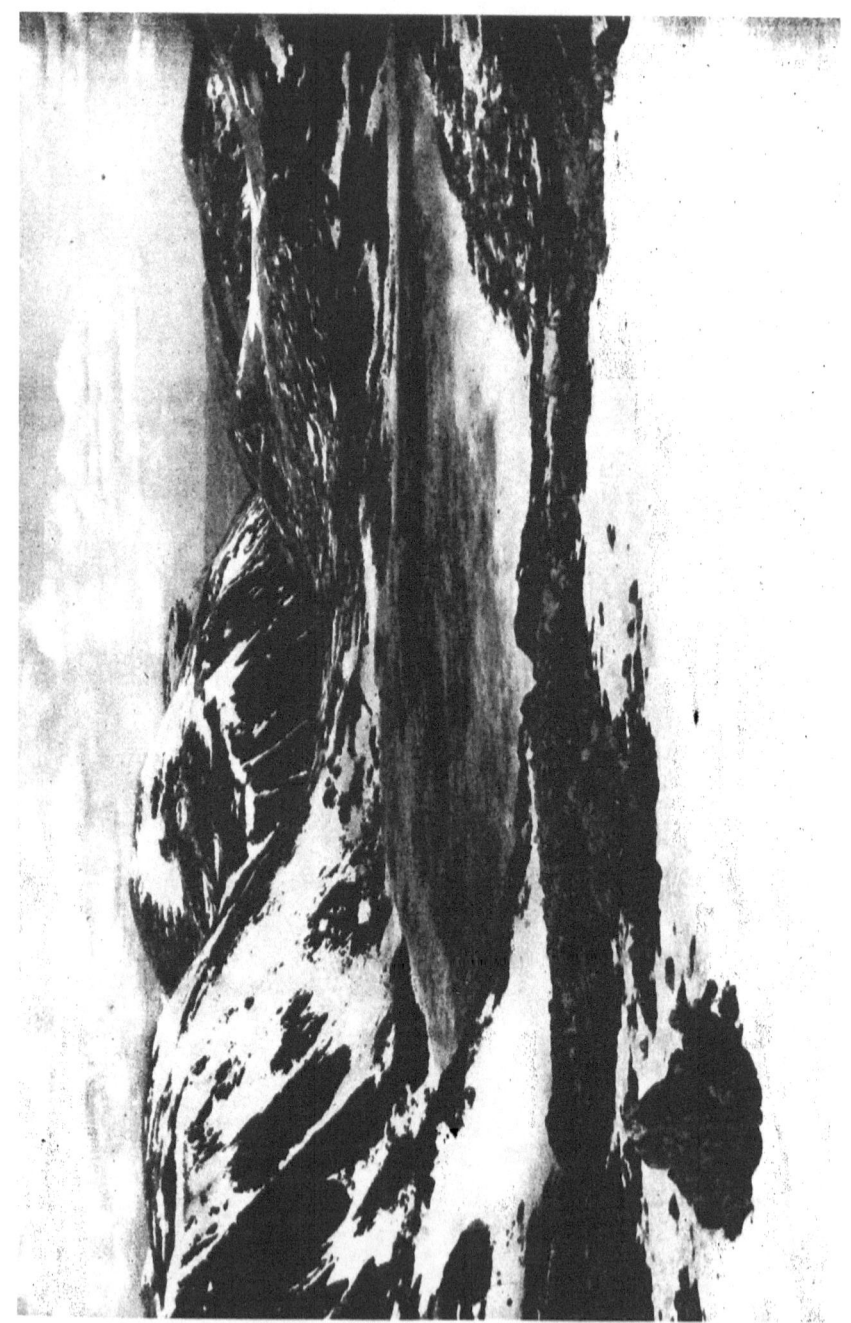

42. DESCENDING COIRE ETCHACHAN TO GLEN DERRY

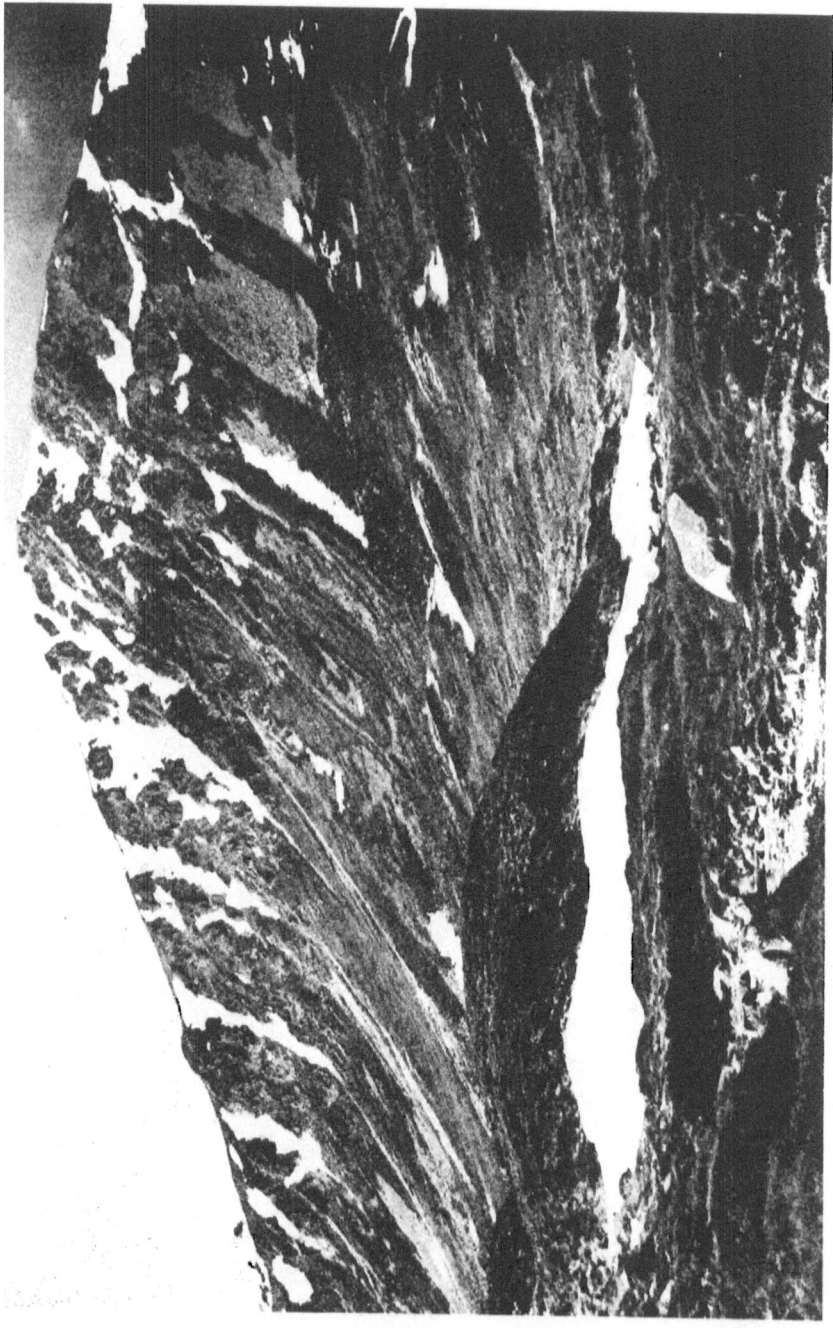

44. LOOKING BACK FROM DERRY WOODS

45. LOOKING TOWARDS THE SNECK FROM GLEN QUOICH

GLEANN AN T'SLUGAIN

This glen runs in a NW. direction from Invercauld House and ends at its junction with Glen Quoich opposite the southern flanks of Beinn a'Bhuird. It is about five miles in length, sparsely wooded in its entirety, and the dreariest valley I encountered. To reach it from Braemar on a bicycle it is necessary to follow the main road to the Old Bridge of Dee where a cart road on the left rises gently through the pines behind Invercauld House. On the other side of it the country is more open and there are attractive views to the west along the wide expanse of Deeside. After passing Alltdourie Cottage, it swings round to the right, threads a band of conifers, and then emerges above the burn in the glen. Beyond this point the road is so bad that cycling is impossible but there is a shorter approach on foot. This involves either crossing the Dee by boat or by wading with a saving in distance of over three miles.

I made two unsuccessful attempts to climb Beinn a'Bhuird and Ben Avon and the shortest route is through this glen. On each occasion the weather was bad and it was during a brief fine period on the second day that I secured these photographs. In the large print, a'Chioch is the characteristic rocky knob of Beinn a'Bhuird rising in the distance above the ruins of Slugain Lodge (46), whilst in the small one taken in the vicinity of Quoich Water, the track in the foreground passes through the dip to the left of Ben Avon and leads to the Sneck, a high ridge connecting these two mountains (45).

46. A CHIOCH FROM SLUGAIN LODGE

THE LAIRIG GHRU

The Lairig Ghru is the finest and most popular of the passes in the Cairngorms and its traverse one of the most arduous walks in the whole of Britain. The best long distance view of it is from Speyside where it appears as a gigantic V-shaped opening between Ben Macdhui and Braeriach. The approaches at either end are full of variety and interest, but the pass itself is the very epitome of austerity, barrenness and gloom. Its passage is not the longest expedition in the district but is enough to test the stamina of the fittest. The distance from Braemar to Aviemore is 27 miles, but it is not everyone who walks the whole way. A lift to Derry Lodge shortens it by 10 miles and another from Coylum Bridge takes off a further two, but the other 15 miles cannot be reduced by any form of transport. A bicycle is a disadvantage rather than an asset. It may even prove a nuisance, especially if you have a heavy rucksack, for the going is of the roughest and the machine will have to be carried, as it is quite impossible to wheel it along the track for most of the way. A point not to be lost sight of by those undertaking this walk is that no accommodation exists between Inverey and Coylum Bridge, a distance of 22 miles. On a fine and warm summer night this is not a serious matter, but in bad weather, not uncommon in the Lairig Ghru, shelter may be urgently required. This may be obtained at the Corrour bothy below the Devil's Point and, in the direst need, a bed might be found at the keepers' cottages at Luibeg or the Linn of Dee; but the risk remains and it should under no circumstances be discounted.

It is a matter of opinion which direction affords the most fascinating walk through the pass; but, personally, I have no doubts about it. It is always an advantage to go from south to north, because on a good day the sunlight reveals the topography of the landscape more clearly. In the reverse direction the sun is not only in one's eyes, but its rays are refracted by the moisture and dust in the atmosphere, when one's full appreciation of the prospect is undoubtedly marred.

Imagine you are going to walk through the Lairig Ghru: first you will see that you are well shod because the track is rough and in places carries much water, and, of course, your rucksack will be well stocked with an ample supply of food to meet any emergency. Possibly you may be able to arrange for transport to Black Bridge but owners of cars do not care to risk the further two miles of bad road to Derry Lodge. Turning to the left across the bridge over the Derry Burn, you will pick up the track which is unmistakable, and opposite Luibeg Cottage a finger-post clearly points the way (49). Hereabouts, if you are lucky, you may see a herd of deer, and you will then turn your back on the last signs of civilisation (50). Steadily ascending the path on the left bank of the stream, you will pass the scattered pines, and if the day is good you will enjoy this prelude to the more strenuous work

[Continued on page 89]

47. DESOLATION

48. THE DEVIL'S POINT AND CAI[RN]

UL FROM LAIRIG GHRU LOCHAN

50. DEER AT DERRY LODGE

52. LOOKING BACK TO DERRY LODGE AND LOCHNAGAR

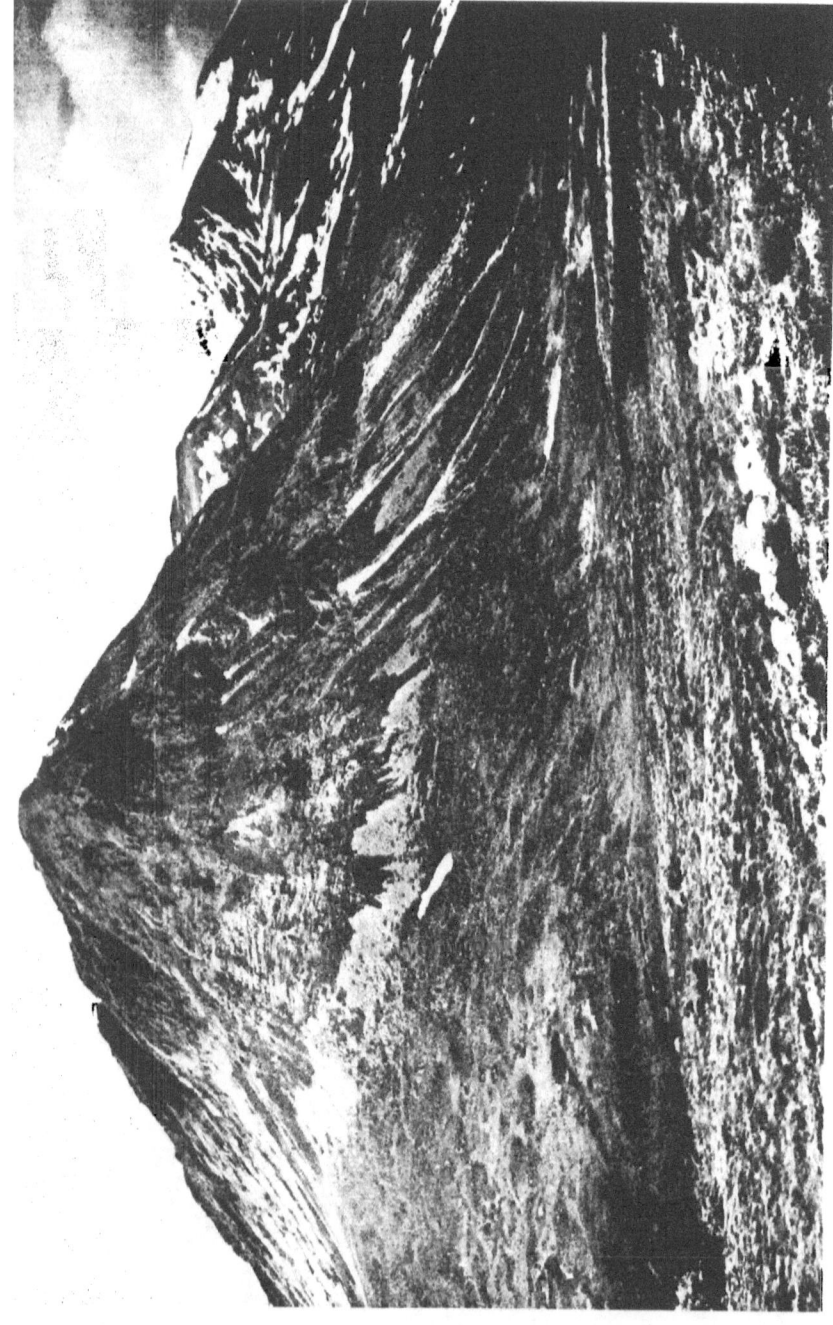

54. LOOKING NORTH THROUGH THE LAIRIG GHRU

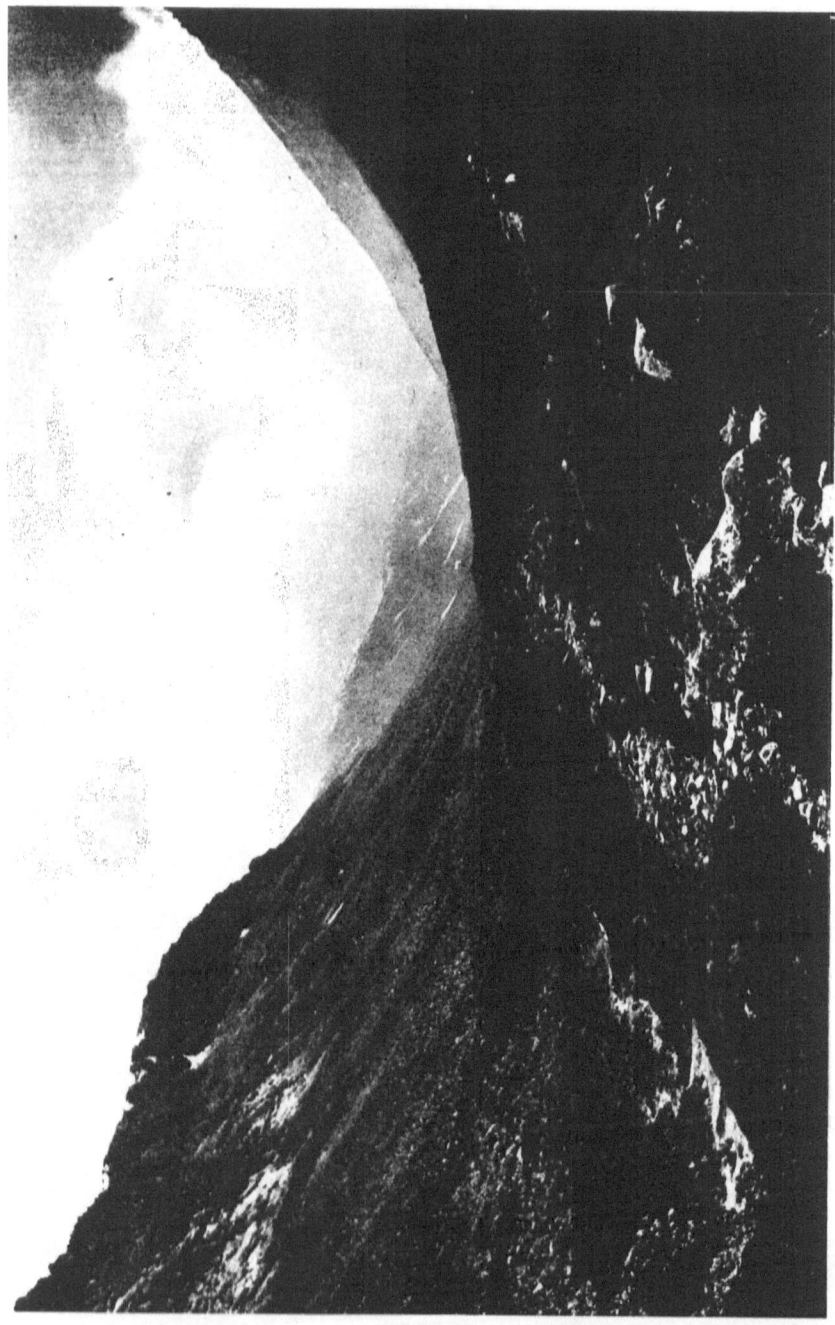

The Lairig Ghru

ahead. In less than two miles you will reach the bifurcation of the paths already mentioned in the ascent of Ben Macdhui where the flat expanse of sand and boulders marks the cloudburst of 1829. Here you must keep to the right if you wish to strike the rather insecure footbridge across the Luibeg Burn, and on looking up the glen to the north you will see Stob Coire Sputan Dearg just to the right of the summit of Ben Macdhui (51). To the west your route is clearly marked as it ascends the rather steep spur of Cairn A'Mhaim, and from the brow of this hill you may look back and scan the hills about Derry Lodge, on the right of which you will perceive the summit of Lochnagar rising above the great expanse of moorland (52).

The going is now easy but rather wet for more than a mile, and as you round the flanks of Cairn a'Mhaim the prospect of Glen Dee and the green floor of Glen Geusachan, overshadowed by Beinn Bhrotain and the Devil's Point, increases in grandeur with every step. Threading the heather on your left runs the Allt Preas nam Meirleach, which rises in a small group of lochans. If you can spare the time, it is worth while descending to see them because they form a charming foreground to the Devil's Point and Cairn Toul, the two superb peaks rising across the glen (48). During this part of the tramp you will have wondered how much farther you have to go before sighting the pass itself, but before swinging round the bend which discloses it, your gaze will be riveted upon the magnificent symmetrical cone of the Devil's Point whose shapely top and rifted supporting crags make such a fine picture of wild mountain grandeur (53). Then, quite suddenly, it will be revealed stretching away interminable to the north and you will doubtless pause to admire its vast proportions. On the left, and just beyond the Devil's Point, the skyline is crowned by Cairn Toul, its flanks sweeping down in one unbroken line past the hanging corrie to the river, 2,400 ft. below. Behind it there is a glimpse of Coire Bhrochain immediately beneath Braeriach, and this merges with Sron na Lairig whose slopes fall towards the pass. On the right the featureless flanks of Ben Macdhui are connected by a high rock ridge whose crest terminates almost overhead with Cairn a'Mhaim (54).

The rough track now drops slightly and then runs almost level for a mile and a half, passing the Corrour bothy on the left between the Devil's Point and Cairn Toul. When you arrive opposite the latter you will realise for the first time the vastness of the distance which separates it from Braeriach, and a little farther along the pass you will see the Angel's Peak high up on the left of the great amphitheatre of An Garbh Coire. If you scan the cliffs forming its crest you may be able to pick out the white line of the infant Dee descending from the Wells of Dee on the summit plateau of Braeriach. Thereafter the pass narrows and on approaching the summit it levels out, being almost choked in places by the large boulders which have fallen from the hill-sides. Here you will encounter the Pools of Dee, whose symmetry deceptively suggests the hand of man, and beyond them you will soon thankfully attain the highest point of the Lairig at an altitude of 2,733 ft.

The descent is gradual for the first mile and a half and then its narrow confines

56. THE FIRST TREE IN ROTHIEMURCHUS

end below the Lurcher's Crag high up on the right. Looking back, the pass presents a picture of wild desolation (55), but this aspect is softened in the advance northwards by occasional glimpses of Speyside far below. The track drops rapidly but there are still over two miles of wilderness to traverse before the first tree heralds the approach of Rothiemurchus (56). Passing through the thick heather you will shortly encounter a small clump of pines standing on top of a little hill. Here you will pause to gaze upon the vast expanse of forest stretching away for miles to the banks of the Spey (57) and frowned upon on the left by the conical sentinel of Carn Eilrig. This coign of vantage is also a good one for the appraisal of the gigantic proportions of the Lairig Ghru, now left behind, where the apparent overhang of the Lurcher is well seen high up on the left (62). If you admire the beauty of trees you will revel in the stately gathering which characterises Rothiemurchus, and if you are fortunate you may catch a glimpse of the little crested tit that lines its nest with deer's hair and makes its home hereabouts. Here and there you will notice

57. LOOKING DOWN ON ROTHIEMURCHUS FOREST

a windswept birch (58), but it is the Scots Pines which are so magnificent (59). After two miles or so of shady forest you will come to the cairn which used to carry the Braemar guidepost, but only fractions of it now lie on this heap of stones. Here the path forks and there are three branches—all unsignposted—so that you may be confused as to which one of them to follow. The right fork goes to Loch Morlich, the middle one to Luineag, some two miles below this loch, and the left branch, your direction, to Coylum Bridge. It descends at first to join the right bank of the Allt Druidh, the burn which rises in the Lairig Ghru, and you advance past its junction with the larger stream of Am Beanaidh coming down from Gleann Einich. You will pass through a deserted clearing in the forest, carpeted with springy turf and garnished by two wooden bridges, and in a short distance reach the iron footbridge erected in 1912 by the Cairngorm Club. This spans the river below a ford, above which a new wooden bridge has been recently thrown across the stream to facilitate the transport of timber (60). To give walkers

58. A WIND-BLOWN BIRCH

an idea of the distances they still have to cover in either direction, the Cairngorm Club thoughtfully placed a tablet on the parapet of their bridge and it gives the following approximate distances and times:

	hours	miles
To Aviemore	$1\frac{1}{2}$	$4\frac{1}{2}$
Coylum Bridge	$\frac{3}{4}$	2
Lairig Ghru summit	3	$5\frac{1}{2}$
Derry Lodge	$6\frac{1}{2}$	14
Linn of Dee	8	18
Braemar	10	$24\frac{1}{2}$

To the north of the bridge the path is unmistakable and there are two signposts some little distance farther on in an open expanse of heather. The left fork leads by Loch an Eilein to Inverdruie and thence to Aviemore, whilst the right one, which is less circuitous, continues by the left bank of the Beanaidh to Coylum Bridge. It passes through a clearing covered with boulders and then picks up the rough road from Gleann Einich which comes in on the left. You may have booked accommodation in this hamlet or be going on to Aviemore. But there is always the chance of a bed at the Dell, which is reached by a path to the left over the bridge. This continues through the forest where juniper and birch blend well with the grand old pines. After a well-earned supper you will doubtless watch the sunset on the distant hills where your travels have led you into the very heart of the Cairngorms (61).

59. THE PATH THROUGH THE PINES

61. SUNDOWN ON THE CAIRNGORMS FROM THE DELL

62. LOOKING BACK TO THE LAIRIG GHRU

4 THE FIRST PINES OF ROTHIEMURCHUS

63. COYLUM BRIDGE

COYLUM BRIDGE

Coylum Bridge might almost be described as the Piccadilly Circus of Speyside, for roads and tracks radiate from it to all the western summits of the Cairngorms. Those marked on the O.S. map are misleading because the sheet only indicates two of them: one running to the west *via* Inverdruie to Aviemore, and the other passing Loch Pityoulish to Nethybridge. Since the last revision, a good road has been constructed past Loch Morlich to Glenmore Lodge, and those giving access both to Gleann Einich and the Lairig Ghru, though carrying a bad surface, should be more clearly shown.

Coylum Bridge spans the River Druie just below the junction of the Luineag and the Beanaidh and is canopied with trees (63), whilst the view from it upstream includes not only the flashing golden water of the burn, but also a graceful overhanging birch whose beauty immediately attracts the eye of every passer-by (64). Loch an Eilein is not far away, but it is necessary first to descend to Inverdruie before taking one of the roads to the left leading to it.

64. GRACE AND ELEGANCE

65. THE DUKE OF GORDON'S MONUMENT FROM THE SPEY

SPEYSIDE

The upper reaches of the Spey as far as Loch Insh are flat and uninteresting, but from this point to Boat of Garten the river winds its way among the hills, and although scarcely as magnificent as the Dee, is resplendent with stretches of great beauty. Below Boat of Garten it again flows through flat country as far as Grantown where the hills close in and the next twenty miles of it afford its most picturesque setting, best seen from the railway which follows its course.

I explored much of Speyside around Aviemore, and although the river is reputed to be most beautiful near Kinrara I found perhaps its loveliest sweep about two miles below. Here it is backed by Tor Alvie, a wooded hill crowned by a monument to the Duke of Gordon, and rising between the river (65) and Loch Alvie (66). Enchanting glimpses of it may also be seen from the road skirting its southern banks between Inverdruie and Feshiebridge, but I found it disappointing just to the north of Aviemore.

The rocky hill of Craigellachie (1,600 ft.) rises on the west of this village and undoubtedly provides the best viewpoint in the vicinity. A small lochan and several cairns decorate its large summit but the finest belvedere is that immediately overlooking the main road and railway. Here the real scale of the country is revealed and the whole mountain range from Cairn Gorm to Sgoran Dubh is brought into proper perspective beyond the vast expanse of Rothiemurchus. This magnificent prospect is seen at its best on a summer evening when the low rays of the sun suffuse the tops and corries with a soft pink glow, whilst the intervening forest is gradually darkened by the relentlessly advancing shadow of the Monadh Liath.

66. LOCH ALVIE

67. LOCH AN EILEIN FROM THE OUTFLOW

LOCH AN EILEIN

    This charming loch, one of the show places in the district, is easily reached by two routes from Inverdruie. The shorter one, favoured by walkers, branches off to the right from the road to Coylum Bridge, while the other, more suitable for cars, turns sharp to the right in the village and after a little over a mile bears to the left at a fork and joins the other rough road near the outflow of the loch. The latter skirts the base of Ord Ban and discloses many a delightful tree study (68).

    Loch an Eilein is overhung by rugged heights and was at one time completely engirdled by forests of pine. But the ravages of the woodcutter have denuded some of the adjacent hills: a feature not fully appreciated until the shore of the loch is reached (67).

    I visited the place on several occasions, but a glorious sunny evening revealed the loch at its best. I followed the grassy road on its western shore and was soon enchanted by the ruined castle standing on a tiny islet not far out in the loch (69 and 70). For many years this was the home of the osprey, eventually harried away by thieving egg collectors. I only had time to walk as far as the keeper's cottage, but beyond it a track continues round the loch, whose circuit may take longer than is expected. Loch Gamhna lies a short step to the south of it and is famous for the water-lilies which blossom in July.

68. A BIRCH BY THE WAYSIDE

70. CAIRN GORM FROM LOCH AN EILEIN

GLEANN EINICH

Gleann Einich, loneliest and most desolate glen in the Cairngorms, extends almost due north-south for five miles to end with Loch Einich, which occupies one of the most impressive positions in the district. It is bounded on the east by Braeriach and its conical sentinel Carn Eilrig, and on the west by Sgoran Dubh and its outlier Cadha Mor. The sombre character of the glen is not disclosed from any of the distant tops, and, indeed, its topography is such that even Craigellachie reveals merely a glimpse of its entrance. It carries the worst road in the district, which ends at the ruins of the upper bothy seven miles from Coylum Bridge, but the preliminary section through Rothiemurchus is passable for cars having a high clearance.

The rough road leaves the main highway by a gate just short of this hamlet and is the same one that leads ultimately to the Lairig Ghru. It first enters the forest and, after leaving the Braemar track on the left, traverses open ground to the east of Whitewell (71). This involves a slight ascent but the road drops again to a small lochan situated at its junction with the Loch an Eilein-Lairig Ghru path (72). The "Locked Gate" here gives access to a fine stretch of Rothiemurchus through which the road rises gently until the Am Beanaidh appears low down on the left. This point is the real entrance to Gleann Einich, and the river, girt with dark pines and hemmed in by the steep rocky flanks of the hills, provides one of the finest scenes in the range. Road and river soon run side by side and the trees gradually thin out until the last sentinels of the forest are left behind (73). Sgoran Dubh now rises ahead but its full stature is hidden by the spurs of Cadha Mor. In a little over a mile the road crosses the burn, and, keeping to its right bank, leads to the lower bothy at an altitude of 1,600 ft. but of which the chimney-stack only remains standing. A track on the left ascends by Beanaidh Bheag to Loch Coire an Lochain, on either side of which rise ridges leading up to Braeriach. This is the shortest route to the summit and involves a climb of three hours from the lower bothy. Loch Mhic Ghille-chaoile lies in a fold of the hills on the opposite side of the glen but is not visible from this point. The road beyond it is in appalling condition and climbs gradually for two miles to the upper bothy at a height of 1,700 ft., which lies in ruins on the hill-side overlooking Loch Einich. A clearly marked path rises to Coire Dhondail on the left and affords an alternative, though longer (4 miles), ascent of Braeriach. On the right a peaty track descends to the loch where the remains of the sluice gates at its outflow are a reminder of the timber-floating days. It continues round the sandy foot of the lake and, skirting its western shore for 1¼ miles, ascends the slopes of Coire Odhar to give easy access to the summits of Sgor Gaoith and Sgoran Dubh. The dark and forbidding cliffs

[Continued on page 110]

71. THE ROAD THROUGH THE FOREST

73. SGORAN DUBH FROM THE LAST TREE IN THE GLEN

Gleann Einich

supporting these tops frown upon Loch Einich far below and the savage buttresses which characterise them provide a great attraction for the rock climber. To explore these crags advantageously, however, it is desirable to camp at the upper bothy and the majority of devotees do so to save the long and tiresome ride from Coylum Bridge.

During my sojourn in Aviemore a strong wind from the west brought almost continuous fine weather but with heavy cloud which usually enveloped all the tops of the Cairngorms. There were brief periods of sunshine but they never persisted throughout the day: a bright morning was followed by a dull afternoon and *vice versa*. On the present occasion, I left for Gleann Einich with the intention of returning over Sgoran Dubh, but the fickle weather let me down; the fleeting sunlight disappeared as I entered the glen and was replaced by low cloud which turned to rain as I reached the upper bothy. I walked down to the foot of the loch where the terrific wind threw spirals of spray high in the air. Long scarves of mist drifted across the great buttresses of Sgoran Dubh and added immeasurably to their height and gloom but it was so dark that I could not see any of their detail. After the long ride up the glen these conditions were dreadfully disappointing. But it was futile to go on farther so I returned to my hotel where a hot bath and a good dinner increased my determination to explore the glen again at the first favourable opportunity.

LOCH MORLICH AND RYVOAN

Loch Morlich lies at an altitude of 1,046 ft. in the wide expanse of Glen More which, in its higher reaches, terminates in the Pass of Ryvoan, a rocky timbered defile leading through to the Nethy. The whole forms a magnificent estate extending to the summit of Cairn Gorm and belonging to the Forestry Commission whose local headquarters are situated at Glenmore Lodge. . A recently macadamised road runs almost all the way to it from Coylum Bridge and only a short section near this hamlet retains its original stony surface. In past decades the forest of Glen More has been severely denuded and there are extensive open spaces of heather-clad moorland between Coylum Bridge and Loch Morlich; but fortunately many glorious pines have been left to fringe its shore. Much replanting has taken place since the first Great War, but it will be years before these saplings assume the grandeur of the rest of the forest.

Loch Morlich is the most delightfully situated sheet of water in the Cairngorms and indeed difficult to rival in the whole of Scotland. Those who expect wildness, severity, and desolation in this landscape will be disappointed, for the dark, though scanty, pines surrounding its foot and the blue rippling waters of the loch, are backed by an extensive forest above which rise three rugged corries, dominated by the fine peaks of Cairn Gorm and Cairn Lochan: an enchanting scene at once proclaiming this loch one of the most lovely in the whole country. A sinuous cart track continues beyond Glenmore Lodge and soon enters a narrow defile, passing the Green Loch on the right (1,174 ft.) and then rising to the dilapidated shelter standing on the crest of Ryvoan (1,288 ft.). On the other side it skirts the foothills enclosing the River Nethy and eventually leads to Forest Lodge where a driving road continues to Nethybridge.

I cycled through Glen More several times and on the present occasion—a beautiful sunny afternoon—I was lucky to see Loch Morlich at its best. Leaving Coylum Bridge behind, I ascended the uphill road, which, on emerging from the first band of trees, reveals a fine prospect of the Lairig Ghru to the south. After crossing the open moorland the road sinks down to the River Luineag which, with its log bridge deep in the forest (75), afforded a charming contrast. Continuing along the tree-lined road I eventually came to the outflow of Loch Morlich where a wooden footbridge spans the stream on the same site as the old sluice gates, whose remains may still be seen in the water. This viewpoint is striking because it is the first place where the hills are revealed in all their glory beyond the glittering surface of the lake. I lingered here for some time fascinated by the play of cloud shadow on those bare bronze slopes. Cairn Gorm dominates the scene on the left and is connected with Cairn Lochan on the right by one of the finest ridges in the whole

[Continued on page 114]

74. THE THREE CORRIES OF THE CAIRNGORM—CAIRN

AN RIDGE FROM THE OUTFLOW OF LOCH MORLICH

Loch Morlich and Ryvoan

range. The late afternoon sun cast its rays deep into the corries: Coire Cas on the left with its long wreath of snow, Coire an t-Sneachda in the centre displaying its shattered precipices to perfection, and Coire an Lochain on the right still carrying some snow on the notorious sloping slab at the foot of its cliffs (74).

I continued on my way with a changing aspect of the loch at every turn in the road; here a stately pine with the long stretch of gleaming sand at the head of the lake (76), there Meall a'Bhuachaille, 2,654 ft., the highest top in the range of hills enclosing Glen More on the north, raising its head above the trees fringing the graceful curves of the shore (77). In due course I came to the gnarled old pine which presides over the long stretch of sand marking the end of Loch Morlich (78), and beyond it ascended the road to Glenmore Lodge. This stands at a splendid elevation and commands views of mountain, loch, and forest, unequalled in the district. I chatted with the keeper who advised me to take my bicycle as far as Ryvoan; but the road was so rough and bumpy that it required all my skill to keep in the saddle. After crossing the burn I had to dismount and wheel the machine nearly all the way to the top of the pass. As I advanced, steep slopes of rock and scree closed in on either side with many lovely pines to enliven the prospect. I left my bicycle near Lochan Uaine and walked over to look upon its green transparent water whose outlet has defied detection (79). Climbing the steeper section of the grass-covered road, I arrived at the crest of the Pass of Ryvoan, where the rain came so suddenly that I was glad to take shelter in the old building, used as a stable in the shooting season. The storm was of short duration and I cycled back to Aviemore in the glow of evening, well content with these varied scenes of mountain splendour.

75. THE RIVER LUINEAG

77. MEALL A'BHUACHAILLE FROM LOCH MORLICH

79. RYVOAN—THE GREEN LOCH—AN LOCHAN UAINE

CAIRN GORM AND CAIRN LOCHAN

Cairn Gorm is the lowest of the 4,000 ft. summits bearing its name, but, owing to its position almost at the northern end of the chain, it commands one of the finest prospects in the district. It is, moreover, the most accessible of the great hills; its ascent is the shortest and easiest, and in consequence the most popular of them all, a fact borne out by the broad well-cairned track rising in an almost direct line from Glenmore Lodge to its summit. From Speyside the mountain has some semblance of shapeliness, although it is rounded and far from striking except when seen from the vicinity of Grantown. If, however, its ascent is combined with the high ridge walk to Cairn Lochan, the cliffs of the latter will make up for any tameness which may characterise its peer.

Every climber is anxious to see his mountain at its best, to select the most interesting route to the summit, and, indeed, if involving a circuit, to take it in the most advantageous direction, because the angle of the sunlight plays such an important part in revealing its topography. A reference to the map will show that while Cairn Gorm is more or less evenly contoured on all sides save its eastern base, Cairn Lochan throws down a steep face to the north-west, and since it will be obvious that this must be in shadow for the greater part of the day, the only chance of observing it under ideal conditions will be in the evening, an hour or two before sunset. In view of these facts, it is preferable to traverse Cairn Lochan after, rather than before, climbing Cairn Gorm, and to complete the circular walk by descending to the west of Coire an Lochain.

After a fortnight on Speyside I had almost given up hope of making this fine expedition, but on the present occasion which proved to be the last day of my trip, the westerly wind was so strong that experience told me it would sooner or later break up the leaden sky hanging over the Cairngorms like a dark shifting curtain. Streaks of blue appeared over the Monadh Liath at noon and this favourable portent induced me to snatch a hurried lunch and, with a well-stocked rucksack, to dash off on my bicycle to Glenmore Lodge some six miles away. The wind was so powerful that I scarcely noticed the long rise to Loch Morlich, and I was more than gratified by the transformation of the heavens where great masses of cumulus were accompanied by an atmosphere of extraordinary clarity.

Leaving my machine near the lodge, I took the well-known path over the river and entered one of the most delightful stretches of forest in the district. I swung along with a light heart and, after crossing the footbridge, was enchanted by the noble pines, the play of light and shadow in the forest, and the music of the burn which here rushes downhill at a great pace (80). I saw a few sheep grazing on the meagre patches of green amid the prolific growth of heather, but there seemed little

[Continued on page 126]

80. THE DANCING CASCADES OF ALLT MOR

81. SHEEP IN GLENMORE FOREST

82. THE LAST OLD PINES IN THE FOREST

84. UP IN THE CLOUDS—THE SUMMIT OF CAIRN GORM (4,084 feet)

or nothing to have induced them to abandon the luscious grassy basin in the rear (81). Where the path forks I took the left branch slanting uphill and had soon left behind the last windswept sentinels of the forest (82). The first thing I noticed on the vast barren slopes of Cairn Gorm was the big perched block, Clach Bharraig. I left the path to climb up to it and on looking back scanned the wide expanse of Glen More below, Loch Morlich forming a conspicuous shining feature in the landscape (83).

The wind on the ridge was so terrific that it almost blew me to the top, for I reached the cairn two hours after leaving the Lodge (84). I found it impossible to stand still and had some doubt whether I could hold my camera steadily enough to get a series of sharp pictures. Great boulders are strewn about the summit of Cairn Gorm and I stumbled over many of them while making for the enormous granite slabs overlooking Loch Avon, whose foot I could see at the base of the steep flanks of Beinn Mheadhoin (85). Retracing my steps, I sheltered behind the cairn while viewing the northern panorama which takes in the whole of Glen More and Rothiemurchus and their respective lochs, backed by the winding Spey, Loch Alvie, and the Monadh Liath. The prospect to the south is not so good since Ben Macdhui and Braeriach block the distant view. I descended the stony western slopes of the mountain in the teeth of the gale, and, on reaching the ridge encircling Coire Cas, had literally to fight my way along it. During the subsequent traverse of Coire an t-Sneachda I was anxious to see its shattered cliffs more closely, but each time I approached the edge of the precipices I was blown clean off my feet by the violence of the wind.

A little *col* separates this part of the ridge from the higher summit of Cairn Lochan (3,983 ft.) and, as this acted like a great funnel, I had a hard struggle to attain the top of the Fiacaill Ridge which comes up on the right. This narrow escarpment forms the eastern wall of Coire an Lochain and is crowned by one of the few spectacular rock *aretes* in the Cairngorms. On reaching it I had the first close view of the sheer cliffs of Cairn Lochan but, since they appeared in silhouette from this point, I pushed on as best I could to the cairn which stands on the very edge of the highest of them (87). Here the force of the wind was phenomenal and it shrieked in wild anger as it tore through the deep gullies which gash the face of the mountain, carrying up with it spray from the two small lochans nearly 1,000 ft. below. Continuing along the edge of the precipices I passed the striking columns perched on the edge of one of the buttresses (88) and after skirting several of these gigantic bastions came to a point on the west of the corrie which clearly revealed their peculiar architecture (86). As I have said elsewhere, the Cairngorm granite weathers in both horizontal and vertical lines, and these cliffs are one of the best examples of the titanic masonry produced by this means. As I climbed down I had to pick my way carefully over the snow and loose boulders but the wind was less boisterous as I lost height and, on looking back, I was able to scan the long line of cliffs in comparative comfort (89). After descending some five or six

85. LOOKING DOWN ON LOCH AVON AND BEINN MHEADHOIN

hundred feet I found another sheltered spot which disclosed an excellent prospect of the whole of Coire an Lochain. On glancing at my watch, I was surprised to find that two hours had elapsed since I left the summit of Cairn Gorm. Although I subsequently tried to find a better viewpoint, this proved to be the most comprehensive because it clearly revealed the two lochans below the long line of engirdling precipices as well as the famous Sloping Slab, a unique feature, partially hidden by the snow at the base of the summit cliffs (90).

I rested here awhile and then descended to the burn flowing down from the two lochans. To the accompaniment of cheerful water music, I followed it for three miles across the heather-clad moorland until I came to a small bothy hidden deep in one of the little glens which open out on to the forest below. It was romantically situated so I entered, opened my rucksack and ate some supper, for, until that moment, I had been so absorbed by the grandeur of the scene that I had completely forgotten the pangs of hunger. It was a delectable spot, shut in on every side by the high banks of the curving glen, and I enjoyed every moment of the solitude, while just beneath the door of the bothy the stream sang joyfully and an occasional grouse flew swiftly by. Donning my rucksack and cameras I then set off down the winding track which crosses a dilapidated footbridge before joining the main path. As I sauntered homewards through the trees, the wind subsided and a strange silence pervaded the forest which, in the dim sunset glow, assumed a new and mysterious charm. I espied Glenmore Lodge ahead, and on reaching it looked back to the scene of my conquest with the clouds gathering about the high hills as the night approached.

86. THE SPECTACULAR ROCK.

TECTURE OF CAIRN LOCHAN

88. THE PINNACLED SUMMIT OF ONE OF THE BUTTRESSES

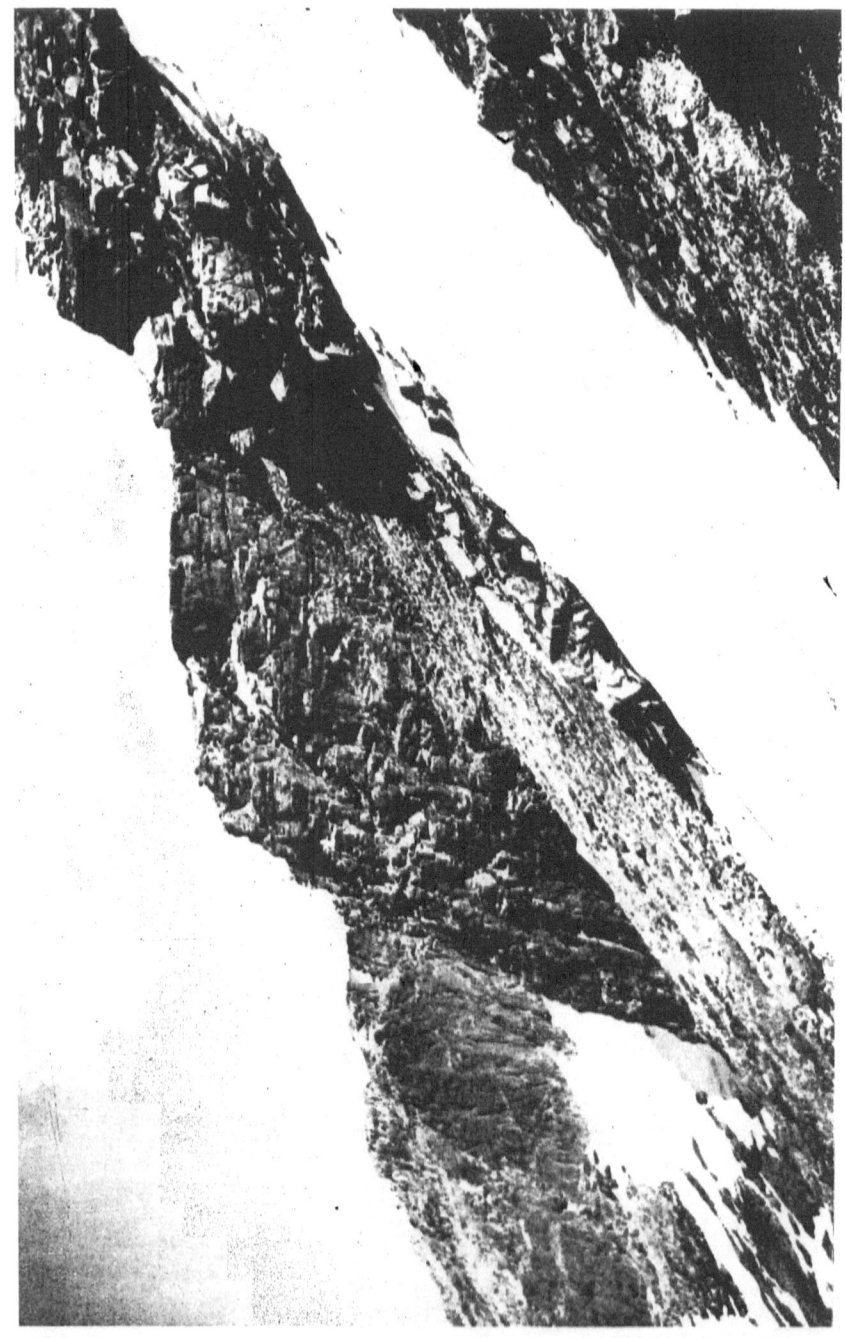

90. LOOKING BACK INTO COIRE AN LOCHAIN
Note the sloping slab above the two lochans

FAREWELL

I mounted my bicycle, and as I ran down from the Lodge, Loch Morlich lay before me, its rippling surface glimmering away faintly in the distance beneath the setting sun. What a change of scene as the evening faded into night! I was so enraptured by the transformation that I dismounted and walked over to the strange little tree that clings tenaciously to the sandy beach. Here I looked across the lake to the cone of Carn Eilrig, now silhouetted against the sky (91), and on turning to the fine old pine on my right, caught the rays of the sun penetrating the heavy banks of cloud to illuminate the little bay, rimmed in deep shadow by the fringing trees (92). I would have liked to have remained here to see the sunset, but as it was getting late I wended my way slowly along the banks of the loch, deeply absorbing every phase of this pageant, so that I could remember it clearly for the rest of my life. On reaching the open moorland, the isolated pines loomed dimly through the gloom and then the sun pierced the cloud again far over the Monadh Liath, to cast its last gleams upon the remnants of the forest before sinking into the Atlantic away to the west (93).

What an appropriate farewell scene for this journey which had taken me into the very heart of the Cairngorms! I had wandered alone through their great solitudes at peace with my Maker and they had given up to me many of their innermost secrets. Though time alone may dim these memories, the vastness, remoteness, and inaccessibility of the smooth bronze hills will never be forgotten; for they are qualities challenging the exploratory spirit in all of us, and in a long day among them we discover the balm for the soul which has to be experienced to be believed.

91. SUNDOWN—CARN EILRIG FROM LOCH MORLICH

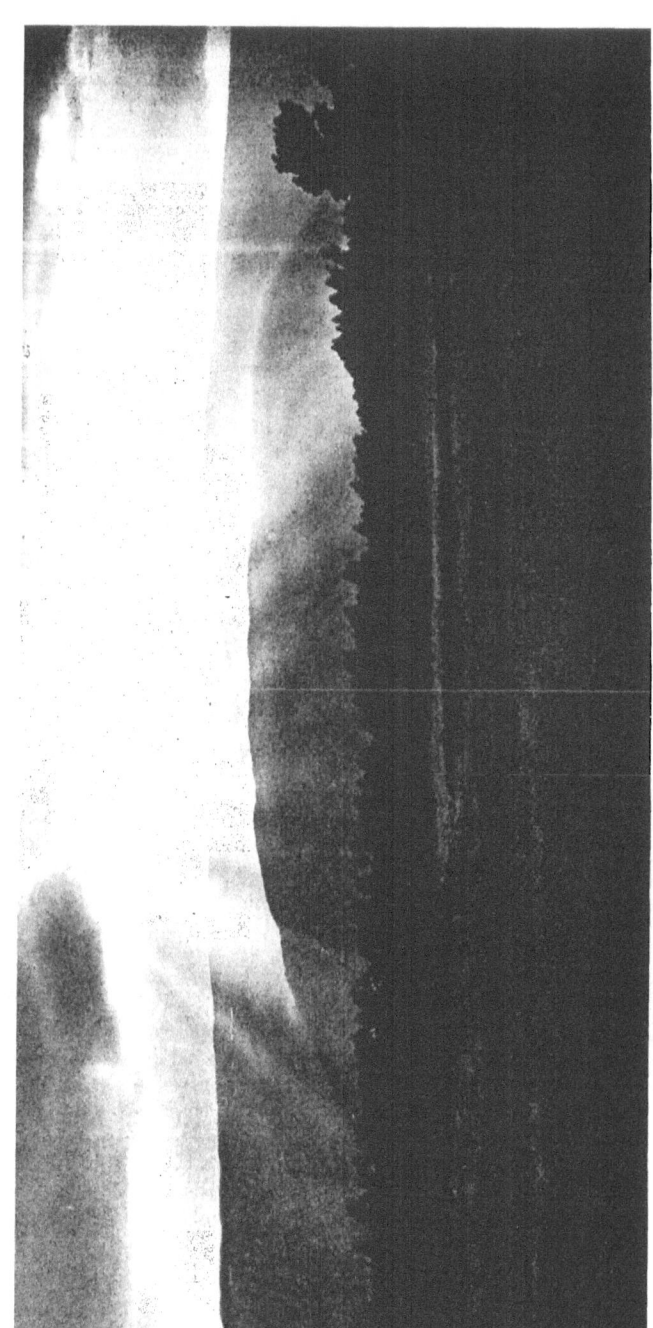

93. ROTHIEMURCHUS—THE SHADES OF NIGHT ARE FALLING

PHOTOGRAPHIC NOTES

When contemplating the present trip I took the opportunity of discussing its chances of success with mountaineers who were familiar with the district. With the one exception of Dr. J. H. Bell, the editor of *The Scottish Mountaineering Club Journal*, their opinions were scarcely encouraging, for, as they said, the hills were smooth and rounded and lacked most of the striking characteristics which make the Western Highlands so attractive and in consequence such good subjects for the camera. I had to admit that most of the photographs I had seen of the Cairngorms confirmed these gloomy views and it was, therefore, with some trepidation that I set out on this tour.

The camera equipment and technique used in the production of this work were identical with that employed for its predecessors, so that a fair comparison may be obtained between the grandeur of the scenery in the Cairngorms and that of the Highlands bordering the western seas. Moreover, the same principles of composition were followed which facilitates this comparison, especially if it is based strictly upon the artistic merits of the prints. Mountain photographers will, therefore, be able to assess the relative pictorial values of the different districts and they will probably come to the same conclusions as I did, namely, that whilst something may be said for the opinions expressed by my friends, most of them evidently concentrated mainly on the climbing and in doing so missed much of the charm of the landscape or else possessed no eye for a picture!

The studies in this volume were selected from over 400 photographs taken on the present tour and are representative of the whole, but had the weather been more favourable throughout, my bag would have been at least fifty per cent greater. The following notes, therefore, include comments upon subjects not contained herein, and I hope they will prove useful and instructive to all those who take their cameras to this magnificent range.

Glen Muick.—The denuding of the forest on the south side of this valley has undoubtedly robbed it of much of its charm, and apart from studies of groups of birch or larch, there is not much of pictorial interest in its lower section. The Linn of Muick could be photographed at its best on a sunny summer morning when the southern bank enclosing the fall would not interfere with the lighting, as it does at other times of the year. Although Loch Muick covers an extensive area, its shores do not bristle with good subjects, but the ground in the vicinity of the Black Burn is worthy of attention. The charming ledges and pools characterising the stream coming down from the Dubh Loch offer all sorts of possibilities, but the loch itself, together with its great overhanging cliffs, demand the photographer's presence very early in the day if he wishes to secure pictures of outstanding merit.

Photographic Notes

Lochnagar.—I should have done better with the double spread of the Corrie had the sky been clear. I was on the summit of the Meikle Pap at the right time, but as I have said elsewhere, cirrus dimmed the sunlight and in consequence there were no brilliant contrasts on its cliffs. More snow would have imparted greater glamour to the whole set of pictures but, apart from these two criticisms, I have no comments to make. Mountaineers who have climbed Lochnagar will agree, I think, that not only is this unfolding panorama comprehensive, but also faithfully portrays this spectacular scene in one of its many moods.

Deeside.—This is full of lovely subjects of which the most popular is the shot of Lochnagar with Balmoral Castle in the foreground. It is a best seller among the postcards, but I did not take it owing to unfavourable conditions each time I was there. Invercauld Bridge is, perhaps, the most picturesque thing on Deeside and I studied it at different times of the day so that I could take advantage of the best lighting. The example included herein was taken during the afternoon, because the most charming aspect of the bridge faces west. Those who like studies of noble Scots Pine will find plenty to keep them busy and there are many delightful stretches of the river fringed with them between Ballater and Braemar. The latter village offers little of note for the camera, but beyond the Linn of Dee there are many interesting spots among which are White Bridge and the Chest of Dee.

Ben Macdhui.—I exposed a large number of negatives during the ascent of this mountain, but obviously I could not use them all as they would in themselves almost make a book. I have included, however, a comprehensive collection which gives a true picture of the peak with its two most popular approaches. I was enchanted by Derry Wood; and the trees here, together with the burn threading the old forest, provide a wealth of scene that would charm the eye of the most hard-bitten professional photographer.

Gleann an t'Slugain.—Frankly, this is not worth a visit unless it is traversed on the way to Beinn a'Bhuird or Ben Avon. The time could be better spent exploring Quoich Water a little farther to the west.

The Lairig Ghru.—I took no less than 62 photographs in this famous pass and whilst I do not claim to have included everything of interest, those who know it will agree I have covered it pretty well. As I have already said, its traverse is a long expedition and mountain photographers know only too well how time can be expended in finding good viewpoints. Under these circumstances a keen amateur might well need two days to walk through it so I would advise him to take care that he is not benighted!

Coylum Bridge.—Apart from the two shots included in these pages, there is nothing else worthy of attention unless it be to snap some of the cottages when conditions are propitious. There are a few attractive scenes in the woods between here and the Dell, but I was unable to find room for them in this book.

Speyside.—I did not cover this region so completely as Deeside, although I took a lot of pictures of the river, Loch Alvie, Kincraig, and Feshiebridge. The lower

Photographic Notes

reaches of the Spey are more picturesque, but when I was there conditions were not conducive of good results.

Loch an Eilein.—From the shots contained in this book it will be obvious that the loch and its environs are resplendent with scenes of photographic appeal. Time may be spent advantageously throughout the day in hunting for subjects in every type and angle of lighting along the whole of its shore.

Gleann Einich.—There is not such a variety of subjects in this glen and its approaches as one might anticipate and the most dynamic shots escaped me owing to the bad weather. I hope to visit it again under favourable conditions when I shall concentrate on viewpoints along the crest of Coire Odhar, because this coign of vantage reveals most perfectly the great cliffs of Sgoran Dubh with the Loch lying in the deep basin far below. Close-ups of the buttresses themselves, taken from the ridge above, should provide many sensational shots.

Loch Morlich and Ryvoan.—The studies of these places speak for themselves and the subjects need no praise from me to increase the esteem visitors will have for them if they go there on a lovely day. Pictures awaiting capture by the camera abound everywhere; but late afternoon is the only time when it is possible to obtain a detailed rendering of the great frieze of hills in the background of Loch Morlich.

Cairn Gorm and Cairn Lochan.—I have already gone into the reasons for taking this walk in the east-west direction, and although I have reproduced only a fraction of my shots, they give a comprehensive picture of everything worth seeing with the one exception of Coire an t'Sneachda. If I climb these hills again on a balmy day I shall make the ascent by way of the Fiacaill Ridge because the rock *arete* itself must be a dramatic subject and in late afternoon also a superb coign of vantage for photographing the shattered cliffs of this corrie. Close-ups of the precipices would be worth taking but the viewpoints depend entirely upon the intrepidity of the mountain photographer. There are, however, the tops of some fine-looking buttresses projecting from the edge on the west side and on a calm day they could be used as foreground interest without much risk.

PHOTOGRAPHIC DATA

Camera Leica IIIa.
Lenses St.=Summitar, 5 cm., f/2.
          W.A.=Elmar 3·5 cm., f/3·5 (Wide Angle).
Filters O.=5 × Orange.
          N.=None used.
Exposures Given in fractions of a second.
Film Material Panatomic X.
Developer D.K. 20 for 15 minutes at 65 degrees F.

Plate Number	Lens	Exposure	Aperture	Filter	Time of Day
Wrapper	St.	1/60	6·3	O·	1
Frontispiece	W.A.	1/60	6·3	O	6
2	St.	1/60	6·3	N	11
3	St.	1/60	6·3	O	3
4	St.	1/60	6·3	O	4
5	St.	1/60	6·3	O	5
6	St.	1/60	6·3	· O	5
7	St.	1/100	6·3	O	4
8	W.A.	1/60	6·3	O	1
9	St.	1/100	6·3	O	4
10	W.A.	1/100	6·3	O	2
11	W.A.	1/60	6·3	O	2
12	W.A.	1/100	6·3	O	2.30
13	W.A.	1/100	6·3	O	2.30
14	St.	1/100	6·3	O	3
15	St.	1/60	6·3	O	3
16	St.	1/60	6·3	O	3
17	St.	1/100	6·3	O	3.30
18	St.	1/100	6·3	O	4
19	St.	1/100	6·3	O	4
20	St.	1/30	4·5	N	11
21	St.	1/60	6·3	O	5
22	St.	1/60	6·3	O	2
23	St.	1/60	6·3	O	3
24	St.	1/60	6·3	O	3
25	St.	1/60	6·3	O	4
26	St.	1/60	6·3	O	6
27	St.	1/60	6·3	O	2
28	St.	1/60	6·3	O	10.30
29	St.	1/60	6·3	O	5
30	St.	1/60	6·3	O	11
31	St.	1/60	6·3	O	10
32	St.	1/60	6·3	O	10.30

PHOTOGRAPHIC DATA—contd.

Plate Number	Lens	Exposure	Aperture	Filter	Time of Day
33	St.	1/60	6·3	O	11.30
34	St.	1/60	6·3	O	1
35	W.A.	1/100	6·3	O	1.30
36	W.A.	1/100	6·3	O	2
37	W.A.	1/100	6·3	O	2.30
38	W.A.	1/60	6·3	O	2.30
39	W.A.	1/100	6·3	O	3
40	W.A.	1/100	6·3	O	3
41	W.A.	1/60	6·3	O	4
42	St.	1/60	6·3	O	4.30
43	St.	1/60	6·3	O	5
44	St.	1/60	6·3	O	12
45	St.	1/30	6·3	O	2
46	St.	1/60	6·3	O	1
47	St.	1/60	6·3	O	1
48	St.	1/60	6·3	O	2
49	St.	1/60	6·3	O	12
50	St.	1/60	6·3	O	12
51	St.	1/60	6·3	O	1
52	St.	1/60	6·3	O	1.30
53	W.A.	1/60	6·3	O	3
54	W.A.	1/60	6·3	O	3
55	W.A.	1/60	6·3	O	2
56	St.	1/60	6·3	O	1
57	St.	1/60	6·3	O	12.30
58	St.	1/60	6·3	O	12
59	St.	1/60	4·5	O	4
60	St.	1/60	6·3	O	5
61	St.	1/60	4·5	O	8
62	St.	1/60	6·3	O	12.30
63	St.	1/60	6·3	N	6
64	St.	1/60	6·3	N	6
65	St.	1/60	6·3	O	11
66	St.	1/60	6·3	O	1
67	St.	1/60	4·5	O	6
68	St.	1/60	6·3	O	5
69	St.	1/60	4·5	O	6
70	St.	1/60	4·5	O	5.30
71	St.	1/60	6·3	O	11
72	St.	1/60	6·3	O	12
73	St.	1/60	6·3	O	1
74	St.	1/60	6·3	O	5
75	St.	1/60	6·3	O	6

PHOTOGRAPHIC DATA—contd.

Plate Number	Lens	Exposure	Aperture	Filter	Time of Day
76	St.	1/60	6·3	O	4.30
77	St.	1/60	6·3	O	4.30
78	St.	1/60	6·3	O	4
79	W.A.	1/60	6·3	O	3
80	St.	1/60	6·3	O	2.30
81	St.	1/60	6·3	O	2.30
82	St.	1/60	6·3	O	3
83	St.	1/100	4·5	O	3.30
84	St.	1/100	4·5	O	4
85	St.	1/100	4·5	O	4.30
86	W.A.	1/60	6·3	O	6
87	W.A.	1/60	6·3	O	5.30
88	W.A.	1/60	6·3	O	5.30
89	W.A.	1/60	6·3	O	6
90	St.	1/40	6·3	O	6
91	St.	1/60	4·5	O	8.30
92	St.	1/60	4·5	O	8.30
93	St.	1/60	4·5	O	9

ANALYSIS: *Lenses* Summitar 73
Wide Angle 21
Filters 5 × Orange 90
None used 4

Index

Accommodation, 14, 21
A'Chioch, 76
Alltdourie Cottage, 76
Allt Druidh, 91, 98
Allt Preas nam Meirleach, 89
Am Beanaidh, 91, 98, 106
Angel's Peak, The, 60, 89
Aviemore, 14, 15, 19, 20, 58, 92, 100, 110

Ballater, 14, 19, 23, 30, 46
Ballochbuie Forest, 46
Balmoral, 30, 46, 139
Beinn a'Bhuird, 34, 46, 61, 76
Beinn Bhrotain, 89
Beinn Mheadhoin, 61, 126
Ben Avon, 34, 76
Ben Macdhui, 58, 60, 89, 139
Ben Nevis, 34, 61
Black Bridge, 19, 58, 61, 78
Black Spout, The, 30, 34
Boat of Garten, 100
Braemar, 14, 19, 23, 58
Braemar Castle, 46
Braeriach, 46, 60, 89, 106
Broad Cairn, The, 24, 25

Cac Càrn Beag, 34
Cac Càrn Mor, 34
Cadha Mor, 106
Cairn a'Mhaim, 60, 89
Cairn Gorm, 58, 61, 111, 120, 126, 127, 140
Cairngorm Club, The, 34, 60, 91, 92
Cairngorms, The, 13, 14, 134
  accommodation in, 14, 20
  approaches and centres, 14, 19, 20
  flora and fauna, 16
  fortnight's pedestrian tour, 22
  geology, 15
  hostels in, 20
  maps, 18
  photography, 138
  weather, 17
Cairn Lochan, 111, 120, 126, 127, 140
Cairn Toul, 60, 89
Càrn Eilrig, 90, 106, 134
Clach Bharraig, 126
Coire an Lochan, 120, 126, 127
  an t'Sneachda, 114, 126, 140
  Bhrochain, 60, 89
  Cas, 114, 126
  Dhondail, 106
  Etchachan, 61
  Odhar, 106, 140
  Sputan Dearg, 60
Corrour bothy, 15, 78, 89
Coyles of Muick, 30
Coylum Bridge, 15, 19, 78, 89, 91, 92, 98, 102, 106, 111, 139
Craigelachie, 100, 106
Cuidhe Crom, 25, 34

Dalwhinnie, 18
Dee, River, 46, 76
Deeside, 16, 30, 46, 139
Dell Hotel, 14, 92
Derry Cairngorm, 58, 61
Derry Lodge, 15, 58, 61, 78, 89
Derry Wood, 61
Devils' Point, The, 46, 78, 89
Distance and times, 19
Druie, River, 98
Dubh Loch, 24, 25

English Lakeland, 13, 25

Feshie Bridge, 100, 139
Fiacaill Ridge, 126, 140
Flora and fauna, 16
Fortnight's pedestrian tour, 22
Foxes' Well, 34

Garbh Allt Falls, 46
Garbh Coire, An, 46, 60, 89
Geology, 15
Glas-allt Shiel, 24
Gleann an t'Slugain, 76, 139
Gleann Einich, 106, 110, 140
Glen Derry, 60, 61
Glen Feshie, 22
Glen Geusachan, 89
Glen Luibeg, 58
Glen Muick, 24, 30, 138
Glen More, 111, 114, 126
Glen Quoich, 76
Glenmore Lodge, 19, 38, 111, 114, 120, 126, 127
Grampians, The, 13
Grantown-on-Spey, 120
Green Loch, The (Lochan Uaine), 111, 114

Invercauld, 46
Inverdruie, 92, 100
Inverey, 19, 46, 58, 78

Kincraig, 139
Kinrara, 100
Kirriemuir, 22

Lairig an Laoigh, 58
Lairig Ghru, 14, 46, 58, 60, 78, 89, 90, 91, 92, 139
Linn of Dee, 46, 78
Linn of Muick, 24
Loch Alvie, 100, 126
  an Eilein, 98, 102, 140
  Avon, 58, 126
  Coire an Lochan, 106
  Einich, 106, 110
  Etchachan, 58, 60
  Gamhna, 102
  Mhic Ghille-chaoile, 106
  Morlich, 17, 111, 114, 120, 126, 134, 140

Loch Muick, 24
  Pityoulish, 98
Lochan Uaine, 60
Lochan Uaine (Ryvoan), 111, 114
Lochend, 24
Lochnagar, 25, 30, 34, 46, 89, 139
Loch nan Eun, 34
Luibeg, 60, 78, 89
Luineag, 98, 111
Lurcher's Crag, The, 90

Maps, 18
Meall a'Bhuachaille, 114
Meikle Pap, The, 25, 30, 34
Monadh Liath, 14, 100, 120, 126, 134
Monadh Ruadh, 14
Morven, 24
Mounth Roads, 20

National Parks, 14, 21
Nethybridge, 98, 111

Old Bridge of Dee, 46, 76
Ord Ban, 102

Pass of Ryvoan, 111, 114
Photographic data, 141
Photographic notes, 138, 139
Pools of Dee, 46, 89

Red Spout, The, 34
Rothiemurchus Forest, 15, 90, 91, 100, 106, 126
Ryvoan, 111, 112, 140

Scottish Mountaineering Club, 19, 138
Sgor an Lochan Uaine, 60
Sgor Gaoith, 106
Sgoran Dubh, 106, 110, 140
Shelter Stone, 58
Ski-ing, 18
Sloping Slab, The, 127
Slugain Lodge, 76
Sneck, The, 76
Speyside, 14, 16, 90, 100, 120, 126, 139
Spittal of Glen Muick, 24, 25, 30
Sròn na Lairig, 60, 89
Sròn Riach, 58, 60
Stob Coire Sputan Dearg, 60, 89
Stuic, The, 34

Tor Alvie, 100

Walking holiday, fortnight's, 22
Weather, 17
Wells of Dee, The, 46, 89
Whitewell, 106
White Mounth, The, 25, 30

Youth Hostels, 14, 22

www.ingramcontent.com/pod-product-compliance
Lightning Source LLC
Chambersburg PA
CBHW021812220426
43662CB00006B/281